INCA &
SPANIARD

BOOKS BY ALBERT MARRIN

The Airman's War
Overlord
Victory in the Pacific
The Secret Armies
The Sea Rovers
War Clouds in the West
The Yanks Are Coming
Struggle for a Continent
The War for Independence
1812: The War Nobody Won
Aztecs and Spaniards
Inca and Spaniard

INCA &
SPANIARD
PIZARRO AND THE
CONQUEST OF PERU

BY ALBERT MARRIN

ATHENEUM   1989   NEW YORK

Atheneum
Macmillan Publishing Company
866 Third Avenue, New York, NY 10022
Collier Macmillan Canada, Inc.
First Edition
Printed in the United States of America
10 9 8 7 6 5 4 3 2 1
Designed by Barbara A. Fitzsimmons

Library of Congress Cataloging-in-Publication Data
Marrin, Albert.
Inca and Spaniard: Pizarro and the conquest of Peru/
by Albert Marrin.—1st ed. p. cm.
Bibliography: p.   Includes index.
Summary: Describes the world of the Incas and how it was changed forever
when the Spanish expedition under Pizarro conquered Peru.
ISBN 0-689-31481-7
1. Peru—History—Conquest, 1522–1548—Juvenile literature.
2. Incas—Juvenile literature. 3. Pizarro, Francisco, ca.
1475–1541—Juvenile literature. [1. Peru—History—Conquest,
1522–1548. 2. Incas. 3. Indians of South America. 4. Pizarro,
Francisco, ca. 1475–1541.] I. Title.
F3442.M44 1989
985′ .01—dc19
88-29372 CIP AC

This book is for my friend
Bruce McMahan

CONTENTS

The Incas governed in such a way that in all the land neither a thief, nor vicious man, nor bad, dishonest woman was known. The men all had honest and profitable employment. The lands and mines, and all kinds of property were so divided that each man knew what belonged to him, and there were no lawsuits. . . . By our bad example we have destroyed this well-governed people. . . . All this I tell . . . to discharge my conscience of a weight, that I may no longer be a party to these things. And I pray God to pardon me, for I am the last to die of all the discoverers and conquistadores . . . and therefore I now do what I can to relieve my conscience.

—Last will and testament
of Mancio Sera de Lajesma
September 15, 1589

INCA & SPANIARD

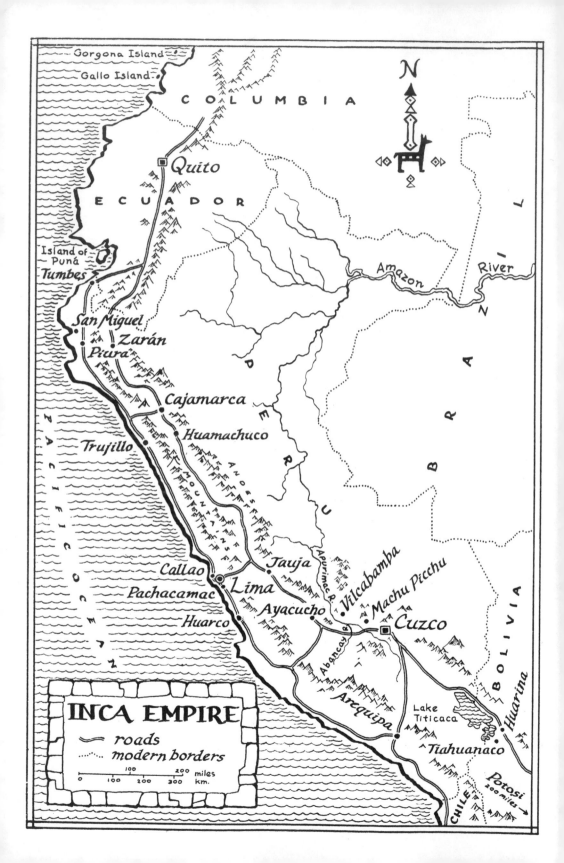

N

Gorgona Island
Gallo Island

C O L U M B I A

Quito

E C U A D O R

Island of Puná
Tumbes

San Miguel
Zarán
Piura

Cajamarca

Huamachuco

Trujillo

P E R U

Amazon   River

B R A Z I L

PACIFIC OCEAN

Tauja

Callao
Lima
Pachacamac
Ayacucho
Huarco

Apurimac R.

Vilcabamba
Machu Picchu
Cuzco

ANDES MOUNTAINS

Abancay R.

Arequipa

Lake Titicaca

BOLIVIA

Huarina

Tiahuanaco

Potosi
200 miles

CHILE

INCA EMPIRE
~~~ roads
····· modern borders

100   200 miles
0   100 200 300 km.

1

CHILDREN
OF THE SUN

IN THE LONG-AGO TIME, THE WORLD WAS WILDER-
ness and mankind lived always in fear and want. There were no
villages or houses or cultivated fields. People were as beasts, shel-
tering beneath rock ledges and in caves. They wore animal skins
or went naked, eating wild plants, raw meat, and sometimes even
their own kind.

One day Inti, Our Father the Sun, took pity upon humanity
and sent to earth his son, Manco Capac, and his daughter, Mama
Ocllo, whom he gave him for a wife and queen. He set the couple
down on Titicaca, the "Rock of the Cat," an island in a lake in
the Andes Mountains between Peru and Bolivia. Lake Titicaca,
which takes its name from the island, is 40 miles wide by 140 miles
long, lying at 12,500 feet above sea level. By day, its icy waters are
the bluest of blues, reflecting the clear sky. At night, when the
stars of the Milky Way sparkle like diamonds on black velvet, the
moon turns the lake to molten silver.

Our Father the Sun gave his children a rod of gold and
entrusted them with a sacred mission. They must set out from
Lake Titicaca in any direction they chose. Wherever they stopped

to eat or rest, they must push the rod into the earth with a single thrust. But each time they did so, it would sink in only a few inches, a sign that this place was not their final destination. One day, however, the rod would be swallowed by the earth. There they must build a city and draw the peoples to it, welding them into an empire to spread the worship of the Sun.

In parting from Manco Capac and his sister-wife, Inti commanded them to rule with justice and mercy. "To the entire world I give my light and my brilliance. I give men warmth when they are cold. . . . Each day that passes I go all around the world in order to have a better knowledge of men's needs and to satisfy these needs: Follow my example. Do unto all of them as a merciful father would do unto his well-beloved children; for I have sent you on earth for the good of men, that they might cease to live as wild animals. You shall be the kings and lords of all the peoples who accept our law and our rule."

Manco Capac and Mama Ocllo headed northward from Lake Titicaca. Wherever they stopped, they tried unsuccessfully to push the gold rod into the earth. Finally they reached the Valley of Cuzco, a fertile valley some twenty miles long and surrounded by snowcapped mountains. When Manco Capac touched the earth with the golden rod, it slipped in easily and disappeared. Here was their promised land!

The royal couple separated to preach their message, he going to the north, she to the south. They told everyone they met that they were Children of the Sun, come from the sky for the good of mankind. Their listeners were astonished, since they'd never seen beings like them. Heavy golden disks were set in their pierced earlobes, and they wore clothes of the softest wool interwoven with golden threads that glistened in the sunlight.

Manco Capac and Mama Ocllo brought their new followers to the valley, teaching them to work together for the common good. He taught the men the skills that were theirs: building houses, selecting seeds, making plows, tilling the soil, irrigating the fields. She taught the women their own special skills: spinning and weaving cloth of wool and cotton, cooking, housekeeping. Above all, they taught the worship of Our Father the Sun.

As the people learned more, they prospered, became happier, and increased in numbers. News of their prosperity spread by word of mouth, drawing others to the valley. The royal couple united them into one people and built their city, Cuzco, the "Navel of the World." Cuzco did, indeed, become the navel, or center, of the Indians' world. For by the time Columbus began his first voyage, it was the capital of the Inca Empire, the richest and most powerful society in the Americas.

The story of Manco Capac and Mama Ocllo is a legend. But like most legends, it contains a kernel of truth. The Native Americans were originally nomads, wanderers, who discovered a new world. About thirty thousand years ago, their ancestors lived in Asia. It was the fourth Ice Age, when glaciers slid down from the North Pole. Moving only a few feet each year, these sheets of ice were often two miles thick and covered thousands of square miles. Nothing stood in their way. Boulders caught beneath them acted as sandpaper, gouging out valleys and grinding hills to dust; the Rocky Mountains were buried, except for some of the tallest peaks. With so much water trapped as ice, the level of the oceans fell by three hundred feet, causing certain shallow areas to emerge from the sea. One of these areas, known to scientists as Beringia, formed a land bridge hundreds of miles wide between Siberia and Alaska.

With the land bridge open, bands of hunters began to cross to the Americas in search of game. The world they discovered teemed with strange creatures. There were beavers as large as grizzly bears, and bears that made full-grown grizzlies seem like cubs. Bison with horns six feet from tip to tip roamed in herds of millions. American lions and saber-toothed tigers preyed upon giant camels and llamas. But none was mightier than the imperial mammoth, an elephant with a thick woolen coat, which stood thirteen feet at the shoulder, several feet taller than the largest African elephant of today.

When the earth warmed again fifteen thousand years ago, the glaciers melted. Beringia vanished beneath the Bering Strait, the northern junction of the Atlantic and Pacific oceans. The Indians were in the New World to stay.

For century after century, they moved southward in family groups or tribes made up of clans, several families tracing their origin to a common ancestor. Some, finding a place they liked, claimed it as their own. Others, arriving too late, or being driven away by those already in possession, continued their wanderings.

Indians reached South America about 10,000 B.C. and began to explore the area we call Peru. Nature has divided Peru into three zones. The first zone, a narrow coastal plain, is a forbidding place. An ocean current flowing from Antarctica sends a stream of cold water rushing northward along the Pacific coast. The current cools the air, sucking the ocean's moisture away from the land. The result is a country where rain never falls; in many places it is so dry that cactus can't grow. Yet amid the reddish brown of the desert are valleys made green by rivers fed by melting mountain snows.

The Andes Mountains, Peru's second zone, loom behind the coast, dominating the horizon as far as the eye can see. The Andes are actually twin ranges, or *cordilleras,* running parallel to each other in a north-south direction. Here the climate varies not with time of year, but with altitude. One can climb from scorching desert at the base of the Western Cordillera to valleys where it is always spring, then to eternal winter on twenty-three thousand-foot peaks. Between the cordilleras is the *altiplano,* or "high plain," a wide tableland covered by short, stubbly grass. Hot by day, frigid by night, the altiplano is laced with streams of solidified lava and studded with stones hurled from volcanoes in bygone ages. In places the plateau is broken by valleys like Cuzco and the basin that holds Lake Titicaca.

Peru's third zone lies beyond the Eastern Cordillera. The high Andes Mountains block clouds blown from the east, forcing them to drop their moisture on the slopes. Hundreds of inches of rain fall there each year. The water runs downhill, forming streams that join to form larger and larger rivers. Eventually these become the Amazon, the world's mightiest river. On its way to the Atlantic, the Amazon tumbles over waterfalls and rushes through the dark, steamy jungles of Brazil.

At various times between 1200 B.C. and A.D. 1000 wandering tribes settled in the coastal valleys of Peru. The Mochica and Chimu lived in the northern valleys, the Nazca and Paraca in the southern. We don't know what they called themselves, since they were "preliterate," that is, without written languages. Unlike the Aztec and Maya, they had no form of writing, not even picture writing. The names we know them by are taken from the places where their remains were discovered.

We know from these remains that they had learned to grow various crops, including chili peppers, beans, maize (Indian corn), and potatoes. They had delicate pottery and colorful cotton textiles for the use of the living in this world and the dead in the next. The dead were placed in sitting positions and wrapped in layers of cloth, with sacred figures of gold and silver placed in the wrappings. The bodies, or "mummy bundles," were then placed in caves or tombs. The desert air quick-dried them, preserving them in perfect condition until their graves were violated by twentieth-century grave robbers.

By the year A.D. 1000 the Mochica and other valley tribes were overcome by the people of Tiahuanaco, a city a few miles south of Lake Titicaca. These people were farmers and herdsmen who depended upon the llama, alpaca, and vicuña for meat and clothing. Although the people of Tiahuanaco originally had migrated from the coast, they were very different from the lowlanders. Air at the higher elevations contains less oxygen than at sea level. The air's thinness makes physical exertion difficult. Over time, however, these mountain dwellers adapted to their environ-

A "mummy bundle" carried to the family tomb. The Inca, together with other Andean peoples, mummified their dead to preserve them rather than bury them in the earth to decay. Mummy bundles often provide modern scientists with valuable information about the past.

ment. They became barrel-chested, with enlarged lungs to take in more air. Their hearts beat slower to use oxygen more efficiently, and their blood became warmer than is normal.

Father Bernard Cobo, a Spanish historian, described them in the late 1500s: "In freezing weather, if you touch their hands, you find them remarkably warm. . . . [T]hey sleep by the road wherever night overtakes them, uncovered to the sky; though . . . snow may fall, they sleep as if in soft beds. I ascribe this extreme warmth to their having stomachs more rugged than the ostrich." When food was plentiful, they stuffed themselves, converting it into body heat. They were (and their descendants are) a short, stocky peo-

6

ple, beardless, with high cheekbones, straight black hair, and copper-colored skin. The men averaged five feet three inches in height, the women only four feet ten inches.

The ruler of Tiahuanaco controlled much of Peru. The city itself was not meant to shelter people, but was built as a religious center. Giant statues, still standing, protected it from evil spirits. The major buildings were temples built on huge stone platforms. When Tiahuanaco began to lose its power, smaller tribes took over the valleys of the altiplano, among these the Colla, Chimu, Charca, and Chanca.

About the year 1250, a tribe calling itself the Inca entered the Valley of Cuzco. We know little about the original Inca, except that they spoke Quechua, "the speech of men," and that their name had several meanings. *Inca*—"lord"—denoted the tribe, the tribe's members, and its ruler, the *Sapa Inca,* or "Sole Lord."

Archaeologists, scientists who study the relics of ancient peoples, think that the Inca's original home was near Lake Titicaca and that they left it in search of better farmland; Manco Capac's golden rod probably symbolizes the plow. Yet the Inca didn't discover the Valley of Cuzco, as claimed in the legend. They were actually latecomers who settled among tribes who'd been there for centuries. Nor is it true that they found the inhabitants living like beasts. At this time all the tribes in the Andes were at about the same level, using the same farming methods and herding llamas.

Still, the Inca *were* different, as their neighbors soon discovered. A tough, arrogant people, they believed that life was a struggle in which one either conquered or was conquered. And they acted upon their belief. Their Sapa Incas were able men who knew how to take advantage of others. The early rulers had such names as War Chieftain, Unforgettable, and He Who Weeps Blood. Under these rulers, the Inca made alliances with other tribes, living up to the pacts when convenient, breaking them when they had something to gain. They threatened and blustered, backed off when necessary, and attacked when they felt certain of victory. As a result, the Inca grew in numbers and power until, by 1438, they held the entire Valley of Cuzco.

In that year, the ninth Sapa Inca began to build a true empire. His name was Pachacuti, meaning "Earthquake" or "Earth Upside Down." The name was well deserved. A brilliant soldier, Pachacuti conquered a swath of territory from Lake Titicaca northward to Ecuador. When he grew too old to take the field in person, he gave command of the army to his son and successor, Topa Inca, the "Unforgettable King."

Topa Inca, who ruled from 1471 to 1493, was probably the greatest war leader ever produced by Native Americans. No one before him, or since, took so much territory in so short a time. Not only did he bring all of Peru under Inca rule, he pushed the boundaries of the empire into present-day Bolivia, Chile, and Argentina. Still not satisfied, he moved northward, conquering coastal Ecuador and the mountain kingdom of Quito.

Topa Inca waged war without mercy. When the coastal city of Huarco resisted too long, he decided to make an example of those who had defied him. He promised the Huarcans fair treatment in return for their surrender. But as they left the safety of their walls, he attacked. Thousands were killed on the spot or hung from the walls; piles of their bleached bones littered the ground for generations.

His son, Huayna Capac, "Young Lord Rich in Virtues," completed the conquest of Ecuador and advanced into what is now the southern part of Colombia.

When Huayna Capac died in 1527, the Inca ruled an empire that stretched nearly three thousand miles from north to south. They called this empire Tawantinsuyu, the "Land of the Four Quarters." They *had* conquered the four quarters of the world; that is, the world of the Andes, the only world they could imagine. They knew nothing of the Aztec and the Maya to the north, let alone the Europeans. With the Mama Cocha, "Mother Sea," to the west and the Amazon jungles to the east, Tawantinsuyu controlled what seemed the whole of the civilized world.

The Sapa Inca and his queen ride in their litter. The Sapa Inca was so holy that he wasn't supposed to touch the ground. The men who carried the litter were chosen for strength and intelligence; if one stumbled, he was instantly killed to prevent bad luck coming to the ruler.

There was no idea of equality in the Land of the Four Quarters. Society was a pyramid, narrow at the top and broad at the base. The Sapa Inca stood at the very pinnacle, alone, glorious, and mighty. As a descendant of Manco Capac and Mama Ocllo, he was regarded by all his subjects—and thought of himself—as divine. His titles were not those of an ordinary ruler, but of a god-king. In addition to being the Sole Lord, he was the "Son of the Sun," the "Magnificent and Unique Inca," and the "Lover of the Poor."

Everything the sun shined upon was the Sapa Inca's. The earth and its waters, the plants, animals, and people belonged to him. Every nugget of gold ("sweat of the Sun") and piece of silver

9

("tears of the Moon") mined in Tawantinsuyu was his personal property to use as he wished. The Indians valued these metals for their beauty, not as wealth.

Coca was even more precious than gold. Coca is a shrub that grows in the humid valleys of the Eastern Cordillera. Nowadays, coca is the basis of a multimillion-dollar drug trade that ruins the lives of thousands each year. The coca leaves are treated chemically to extract cocaine, which can be sniffed or smoked as "crack." However it is used, cocaine changes the chemistry of the human brain, causing addiction, permanent damage, and often death. Chewing dried coca leaves, however, is less dangerous, since it releases only tiny amounts of cocaine into the body. Long before the coming of the Inca, the Andean Indians discovered that chewing the leaves of the coca bush made them "high"; a mouthful of coca leaves enabled workers to resist hunger and fatigue. Under the Inca, coca production was a royal monopoly. All plantations belonged to the Sapa Inca, who allowed only his favorites to chew the leaves. The royal family and the nobility used them regularly. The greatest honor was to receive a mouthful of coca leaves from the jeweled bag that the Sapa Inca wore at his side.

Tawantinsuyu was a dictatorship that obeyed the will of one man. The Sapa Inca's word was law, and there was no appeal from his decisions. His hand gave life as well as death. To be touched by him was a blessing; yet he had only to lift his hand for the greatest nobleman to be killed instantly. Whenever the Sapa Inca passed, people knelt and touched their foreheads to the ground, because ordinary mortals were unworthy of seeing him. The most important visitor could only approach him after removing his sandals and placing a light sack or bundle of twigs on his back as a sign of submission. No one dared look the Sapa Inca in the face.

The Sapa Inca lived in ease and luxury. His costume was unlike any in Tawantinsuyu. He wore a tunic of the finest cloth studded with jewels; some clothing was even made of the fur of vampire bats woven into a light, silky fabric. Plugs of gold three inches wide were set in his pierced ears, and a large golden disk, symbol of the Sun, covered his chest. His "crown" was a band of woolen cords of different colors, with red tassels hanging through little gold tubes over his forehead. On his feet were golden sandals, and he sat on a low stool set on a platform of solid gold.

During meals, the Sapa Inca sat on his stool surrounded by bowls of gold, silver, and pottery placed on little mats. His servants were his wives, who catered to his every whim. He'd point to a dish, and a wife, bowing, held it in her hands while he ate. If there was something he didn't like, he'd spit it into another wife's hands. If any food fell onto his clothing, he went into his rooms and changed before continuing the meal.

Everything he touched required special treatment. At the end of the meal, all food remnants—bones, gristle, corncobs—were stored in chests in a building near the palace. Each day's clothes were also stored there, for he wore a garment only once. All was burned at year's end and the ashes scattered to the winds. For the Inca this was not wasteful, but prudent. They believed that whatever has belonged to a person always remains part of him. A nail paring, hair, a sandal, a fruit pit, even spittle, could be dangerous in the wrong hands. An enemy could attach the item to a doll representing the Sapa Inca, which the enemy would "torture" or "kill," thereby harming the ruler himself. It is for this reason that any hairs that fell on the Sapa Inca's clothing were removed and eaten by the royal women.

The Sapa Inca practised polygyny and incest. Polygyny, a man's having more than one wife at a time, was found among many peoples in the Old World and the New. Incest, having sex with a close relative, is forbidden by nearly all peoples and has been punished by death.

Incest was part of the origin of the Inca people. As we've seen, Manco Capac and Mama Ocllo were at once brother and sister, husband and wife. Even so, for many years their descendants found wives among the daughters of local tribal chieftains. Beginning with Pachacuti, however, the Sapa Incas married their

Attended by her ladies, the coya, "queen," washes her hair. These ladies were no mere servants, but daughters of the nobility. Although not a goddess herself, as the wife of a living god, the queen was entitled to all the honor and respect due to the Sapa Inca.

sisters. Like the pharaohs of ancient Egypt, they did this in order to preserve the "purity" of the royal blood.

Although the Sapa Inca could have as many wives as he pleased, only his eldest full sister could be *coya,* queen. She, too, wore a crown of woolen braids and sat on a stool-throne. All the respect due her husband was also due to her. But in addition to his coya, the ruler had any number of secondary wives. These were all his half sisters, his father's children by any cousins and women of the nobility who attracted his attention. The Sapa Inca might have hundreds of children, but only his sons by the coya could inherit the crown. Unlike a European king, whose heir was always the firstborn son, the Sapa Inca chose only the ablest to take his place.

The Sapa Inca never really died. When he came to the end of his time on earth, the Sun called him to the sky. Yet he never went on his journey alone. The Inca believed that the spirits of the dead had the same needs as when they had inhabited bodies of flesh and blood. As the Sapa Inca was served in life, so must his spirit be served in death. Nooses were hung in special places so that wives and servants wishing to share his glory could commit suicide. Many died, eager to live forever in the Sun's golden rays. Some, who were less eager, were drugged with coca and strangled.

The Sapa Inca's body, like that of an Egyptian pharaoh, was mummified to prevent decay. After the intestines were removed, the body was treated with herbs and dried in the sun, which made it hard as wood. It was then dressed up, golden disks fitted into the eye sockets, and brought to the emperor's favorite palace. There it sat on a throne with bowed head as if deep in thought. The mummy was pampered as if it might return to life at any moment. Servants hovered around it day and night, serving it meals, bringing it coca, and entertaining it with the latest gossip. Women wearing golden masks stood on either side to brush away flies with feather fans. When the coya died, she was mummified and seated alongside the Sapa Inca's mummy. During festivals, the royal mummies were paraded through Cuzco and set up at a banquet given in their honor.

The Sapa Inca ruled with the help of the nobility, who were usually his relatives. Nobles held the highest offices: governors of provinces, ambassadors, judges, priests. They formed the emperor's bodyguard and led the army as generals. They were expected to do their duty honestly and well. There was no excuse for failure, let alone disobedience, and both meant certain death; Topa Inca killed his own brother, a general, for advancing against orders, even though he'd won an important victory.

In return for their services, nobles paid no taxes and could have several wives. This was a real privilege, for the number of a man's wives was a sign of wealth and respect.

Young noblemen attended the House of Learning, the Inca version of a university, for four years. There *amautas,* "wise men," taught them Inca customs, history, law, religion, poetry, and music. Famous warriors taught the use of weapons and put the

An Inca "accountant." The Inca used the quipu, knotted strings of different lengths and colors, to keep accurate, detailed accounts of everything from newborn babies in a village to the amount of maize kept in government storehouses.

noblemen through daily physical exercises. Those who fell behind were hit ten times on the soles of the feet with a paddle. That may not seem like serious punishment—to one who has never experienced it. But the soles of the feet are very tender, and every blow sends a current of pain through the body.

One of the most important subjects taught was the *quipu,* the lore of the knot. Although the Inca lacked writing, they were able to keep accurate records. The quipu was a long rope from which dangled colored strings, each with its own meaning. Yellow stood for gold, white for silver, green for coca, red for soldiers, and so on. Each string was tied with combinations of knots, which, taken together, gave a picture of the empire at any given moment. Officials could tell the Sapa Inca how many warriors he could expect from any village, the food available to feed them, and where it was stored. If there was a poor harvest in one province, they knew at a glance how much help its neighbors could send. Knots representing births and deaths were constantly being tied and untied; quipus even recorded the ages of the population and the number of people following each occupation.

14

To graduate from the House of Learning, one had to pass final examinations that were pure torture. For a week, a would-be graduate fasted and raced up and down mountain slopes, cheered on by beautiful girls offering coca leaves. He fought sham battles with real weapons and sometimes died. Such a death was worthy of a noble youth, a credit to his family. One who flinched or cried out in pain disgraced his family and became an outcast. Those who succeeded knelt before the Sapa Inca to have their ears pierced with a golden needle. Heavy earplugs were inserted, which gradually enlarged the lobes until they reached to the shoulders. The House of Learning turned out tough, able men ready to give their lives for their master.

It was different for the *purics,* the ordinary Indians who were in the majority in the empire. Nothing that concerned them was really private. The Sapa Inca's rules touched them in the most intimate details of their lives. Should they marry? Who? When? Where would they live? These and hundreds of similar questions were decided, not by the purics themselves, but by the Sapa Inca and his officials.

There were no Inca bachelors or spinsters, since all married whether they wanted to or not. Marriage was not a matter of love, but a duty to the state. Large families were the Sapa Inca's most precious resource. They meant more workers, greater wealth, and larger armies.

The Sapa Inca ruled that the puric could have only one wife, chosen only from his village. On a given day an official known as He Who Sees Everything came to the village carrying its quipus. The knots contained all the information he needed, and there was no avoiding him. Unmarried men of twenty-five and women of eighteen were ordered to appear before him. After arranging them in two rows, he asked if any had decided to marry. These couples stepped forward, joined hands, and were declared husband and wife. The others were paired off by He Who Sees Everything. "You take this one; you take that one," he'd say, and that was that.

INCA AND SPANIARD

The government, which owned all the land, gave the newly-weds two sets of new clothes, two pairs of sandals, and assigned them a plot of land to farm. Each year the village lands were distributed, not in equal shares, but according to family size. Couples gained land with the birth of each child, lost land as children died or married and set up their own families. No family, be it noble or puric, received more than enough land to support itself. There were no exceptions.

Even the handicapped were full members of the community. Like everyone else, they had to marry within their own group. The blind married the blind, the deaf the deaf, the mute the mute; even the retarded had to marry. They also received land and were expected to work as far as their abilities allowed.

A commoner lived in a one-room stone hut, windowless, with a thatched roof. Dark and damp, it stank of sweat, urine, and manure. Human and animal wastes were saved; women washed their hair in urine to kill lice, and manure was used as fertilizer. The hut had no chimney, so smoke from the dried llama dung burned in the cooking fire escaped through the thatch. Guinea pigs scampered about until their turn came in the cooking pot. "Furniture" was a couple of wooden hooks set in the wall and two or three earthenware pots. There were no chairs; purics squatted on the ground. The family slept on llama skins spread on the bare floor. Everyone shared the same bed, and youngsters learned the facts of life early. There was no effort at privacy; since their activities were natural, parents thought privacy unnecessary.

The Inca woman was a combination wife, helper, and beast of burden. First her father, then her husband, was her lord, just as the Sapa Inca was lord of all. "She was a thing," wrote a Spaniard after the Conquest, "and could be treated as such." She'd been born to work, and work hard, so long as she lived. Up before dawn, she worked without letup until bedtime. She collected firewood, cooked meals, mended clothes, cared for farm animals, looked after her children, and helped her husband in the

16

fields. When she walked outdoors, if her hands were free, she spun cotton and wool into thread. She seemed always to be chewing and spitting. The Inca's favorite drink was *chicha,* a beer made from maize. Women chewed maize kernels into a mush and spit it into jars of warm water, where their saliva converted the mixture to alcohol.

Childbearing couldn't interfere with work, and a mother-to-be worked throughout pregnancy. When her time came, she delivered her baby without the help of doctors or midwives and went back to work. This amazed the Spaniard Pedro Pizarro. Indian wives, he wrote, "were very submissive to their husbands, so much so that the mountain women were loaded and carried burdens like the men. . . . If it happened that, while traveling along with a burden, they gave birth to a child, they went aside from the road in order to lie in, and afterward they went to where there was water, and they washed the babe themselves, and then they took it and threw it on top of the pack they were carrying and went on traveling. I saw this several times."

Returning home, the mother put her newborn into a cradle and tied blocks of wood to the baby's forehead and the back of its head. These blocks were gradually tightened, until the baby's forehead sloped backward. A sloped forehead, especially in women, was a mark of beauty among the Inca.

The Inca were loving parents, but firm ones. Life was hard, and the puric child had to get used to discomfort from the start. A nursing mother merely leaned down over her child, without taking it in her arms. Infants were never hugged, or fondled, or taken on the lap, or played with, for fear of making weaklings. Children were left to cry until they stopped by themselves. When the child outgrew its cradle, the mother put the child in a hole in the ground up to its chest and left it to amuse itself however it could, but on no account did she take the child in her arms. Its bathwater was warmed in her mouth and squirted over its body. If the child got sick, she daubed it with urine, which served as a

A child whipping a top. Although they worked hard, Inca children also enjoyed various games.

mild disinfectant. She removed lice with her fingers, crushing the tiny insects between her teeth.

For the first years of life, children were simply called *wawa*—"baby." At five, a baby's hair and fingernails were cut for the first time and it received a name. Boys were named for animals and warlike things: Puma (mountain lion), Falcon, Hawk, Serpent, Dagger, Siege. Girls had more delicate names: Star, Coca, Blue Egg, Halo, Darling, Happy, How Beautiful.

Unlike the educated nobles, purics were deliberately uneducated, since the rulers feared that learning would make them proud and rebellious. It was enough for puric boys to follow their fathers' trades and girls to copy their mothers. Teaching was the obligation of parents, who were held responsible for their children's actions. If a child got into trouble, it was because the child hadn't been properly taught at home. That was the father's fault, and he was punished instead.

The growing youngster learned that, for the puric, being unfree was the central fact of life. Proof of this was brought home to him every day. He saw, for example, how He Who Sees Everything pried into everything in the village. Hut doors had to be left open during the day. When a messy housewife was discovered, she had to eat the dirt of her house in front of the whole village. The growing youngster learned that he must spend his whole life

18

in the village of his birth, unless the Sapa Inca decided otherwise. He must wear the traditional costume of his province—to make him stand out if he left home without permission. Above all, he must never, ever, think for himself. The government thought for him. All he had to do was be humble, quiet, and obedient.

Disobedience called forth the full fury of the law. Inca law was simple, its basic ideas captured in a short sentence: *Ama sua, ama llula, ama cheklla*—"Do not steal, do not lie, do not be lazy." The Sapa Inca never made laws just to frighten people. They were made to be enforced. His justice was sure, swift, and terrible.

Those accused of crimes had a trial as fair as any in the world at the time. Witnesses gave evidence and the accused was allowed to defend himself. There were no lawyers, as the judge was trusted to give a just verdict after hearing the evidence. Those who were found guilty weren't sent to prison, nor did anyone try to reform them. They paid with their blood or their life. It was that simple.

Punishment was carried out in public as an example to others. Gossipers were whipped until their bodies were covered with ugly red welts. Thieves were whipped for the first offense; the second offense cost an eye, a hand, or a foot. Three-time offenders were hanged by the feet, dying painfully as the blood rushed to their heads. Murderers were hung, stoned, or flung off a cliff. The law also protected valuable plants and animals. Fruit trees, timber trees, llamas, and other animals could be destroyed only with the Sapa Inca's permission. Those who acted on their own paid with their lives.

Judges and government officials, being nobles, were held to a higher standard than ordinary citizens. If a judge gave an unfair decision, or an official took a bribe, usually he was killed and his family disgraced. At the very least he suffered the *hiwaya;* a big stone was dropped on his back from a height of three feet, which might or might not be fatal.

Prisons were only for war captives and those who challenged the Sapa Inca's authority. On his personal orders, traitors, rebels, and spies were kept in an underground prison in Cuzco. Known as the Place of the Pit, it was as close as one could get to hell and still be alive. It consisted of a maze of tunnels and pits lined with razor-sharp flints that allowed prisoners no place to rest; if they dozed off, a painful cut awakened them at the slightest change of position. Besides the usual tortures, prisoners were kept in constant terror by poisonous snakes, scorpions, spiders, and hungry pumas, which could be let into their cells at any moment. Few left the Place of the Pit either alive or sane.

All the Sapa Inca's subjects worked. The nobles did the "brain work," organizing and supervising whatever needed to be done. The common folk worked in the fields and at their trades. Even the blind were kept busy, stripping the kernels of maize off the cob. Only the very old, the sick, and the disabled were excused from work, and they were supported by the state. The Inca saw themselves not as individuals responsible only for themselves, but as part of a greater whole, the community. Everyone was entitled to community help, just as everyone had to help others in need. If a person couldn't handle a task, he wasn't ashamed to call upon his neighbors. Being lazy, however, was the same as stealing, since the lazy robbed the community of their labor. Those found guilty of laziness were clubbed to death.

The Sapa Inca would have agreed with the saying, "Idle hands are the devil's tools." He understood that people with free time might criticize the government, and that couldn't be permitted under any circumstances. If there were no useful projects in an area, he made busywork. One Sapa Inca is said to have ordered a hill moved from one place to another, just to give the people something to do.

As soon as children could understand the meaning of words and use their hands, they were given simple tasks. Those under five were set to picking up twigs and catching lice. Young boys between five and ten chased birds away from the fields. Ten- to eighteen-year-olds tended the llamas, and from eighteen until marriage they worked alongside their fathers as farmers.

20

Boys wore animal skins and twirled slings to frighten birds away from the newly planted crops.

Farming in the Andes required patient, backbreaking labor. Making the soil yield its bounty was a struggle in which success was as sweet as any victory in battle. As they plowed, farmers chanted the word *haylli*, "victory":

> The men:
> *Ho! victory. Ho! victory.*
> *Here digging stick, here the furrow!*
> *Here the sweat, here the toil!*
>
> The women:
> *Huzzah, men, huzzah!*

21

Planting maize. The Inca men used the simple "foot-plow" to make a hole in the ground. The women tossed in the maize kernels.

Andean valleys are narrow and steep, limiting the amount of flat bottomland. What there was had to be given loving care. Villages were built on mountainsides to save bottomland for farming. When more land was needed, it had to be stolen from the mountains themselves. The Inca, like earlier settlers, were masters at terracing; that is, carving rows of giant steps up a mountainside and supporting them with stone walls. Inca terraces were built to last, and many, covering as much as 250 acres each, are still in use.

But land must be watered and fertilized in order to be productive. There is plenty of water in the Andes—from lakes, streams, glacial runoff—if one knows how to get it to the right place. The Inca knew. Without iron tools or explosives, they cut channels as much as sixty miles long through solid rock, passed

22

them through tunnels, and sent them across valleys on aqueducts that the Romans might have envied. Although their only fertilizers were human and animal manure, they were lucky to have an unlimited supply of the best type: guano, the droppings of sea-birds, mostly sea gulls. For thousands of years, huge flocks of birds nested on the offshore islands of Peru, forming mountains of solidified manure. To the Inca these islands were more precious than gold mines. The Sapa Inca allowed each province to take only a fixed share of guano at certain times of the year. Anyone who killed birds or disturbed them while nesting was put to death. Today guano is one of the most valuable exports of the Republic of Peru.

The Inca grew an amazing variety of crops. Fully half the plant foods eaten in the world today were developed in the Land of the Four Quarters. Sweet potatoes, squash, chili peppers, beans, and gourds were raised on the hot desert coast. Peanuts, cashews, chocolate, pineapples, and maniocs, the source of tapioca, grew in the Upper Amazon, which the Inca controlled. But nature's greatest bounty came from the mountain valleys: soybeans, squash, tomatoes, mulberries, pumpkins, avocados, papayas, guavas. Twenty varieties of maize, the Inca's chief food, grew at different altitudes. Chewed maize became chicha and ground maize was baked into bread. Maize kernels were made into popcorn, developed and prized as a delicacy by the Inca. Next to maize, the Inca depended most on the potato. The Inca had forty varieties of potato, or *papa,* ranging in taste from sweet to bitter. Papa came in a rainbow of colors: yellow-white, pink-gray, brown, tan, purple, black, spotted, streaked. Since storage space was limited, the Inca invented dehydration for keeping large quantities without spoiling. Potatoes were left overnight on the ground to freeze, and, after thawing in the morning sun, the water was squeezed out by people stomping on them. The process was repeated several times until all that remained was a white flour that could last for years.

INCA AND SPANIARD

In addition to their fields, the Inca kept herds of llamas. The llama was their largest and most important animal. They slept on its hide, wove its wool into cloth, cooked with its dung, and ate its flesh. Llama meat was eaten fresh or as wind-dried strips called *charqui*—pronounced "jerky" by Europeans. Surefooted and un-afraid of heights, the llama could carry loads of up to 110 pounds. But a heavier load caused it to lie down and spit in its master's face. Since the llama couldn't bear a man's weight, the Inca either walked or, like the Sapa Inca, were carried on a litter.

Much of the commoners' time was spent in paying taxes. Inca taxation was unlike any in the world. Other peoples are taxed on their personal property, paying in money or goods. The Inca paid in labor and time. In addition to their own fields, farmers had to work the lands of the Sapa Inca and the priests. Craftsmen—goldsmiths, stonemasons, sculptors, potters, weavers—worked on materials provided by the government, handing over the finished product. Others labored in the mines or built roads, temples, and fortresses for a fixed number of days each year. At villages near important river crossings, all the men turned out to build and repair bridges.

The labor tax was no hardship, for everything the people produced came back to them in one way or another. Fortresses lent protection, as did roads and bridges, necessary for moving warriors around the empire. Only a small amount of the goods produced were used by the Sapa Inca and the priests. The rest was kept in government warehouses to be used as needed. Warehouses were scattered throughout the country, so that even the smallest village had one nearby. These were filled with maize, charqui, potato flour, dried vegetables, sun-dried fish, rope, salt, wool, cotton, clothing, sandals, and powdered dyes ready for use. There were also rooms for the feathers of hummingbirds obtained from the Indians of the Amazon. War materials—weapons, tents, shields, and mounds of sling stones—were stored in special ware-houses.

24

The keeper of the quipu, right, tells a government official just what is stored in a royal storehouse and in what amounts. This system prevented hardship in times of shortage and guaranteed that everyone, no matter how humble, received a fair share.

Certain warehouses always kept a ten-year food reserve. If there was a crop failure, food was distributed free of charge, so that none need starve. (Compare this to Europe, where there were no government reserves and most countries were struck by famine every couple of years.) There was no such thing as charity, because the needy received back what they'd produced with their own hands. Beggars were unknown in the Land of the Four Quarters until after the Spanish conquest.

The Inca paid taxes not only in work and time, but in young girls. Every year as many as six hundred girls aged eight to twelve were chosen from each province of the empire. These girls, known as Chosen Women, had to be intelligent and pretty. They went willingly and with their parents' blessing; to have a daughter in the service of the god-king was an honor for a humble family.

Once selected, girls were sent by the governor to a local House of the Chosen Women. This building, gray, fortresslike, and guarded by soldiers, was off-limits to men; anyone caught near the wall was instantly hung by the feet. The girls were forbidden to leave for any reason, even a parent's death. Every waking moment was supervised by matrons ready to punish the slightest offense. Every day, all day, was spent in learning religious rituals, chewing maize kernels, making fine cloth, and sewing the Sapa Inca's clothes.

At the end of three years, an inspector picked the best girls to be sent to Cuzco. There the Sapa Inca divided them into three groups. The first group became his own property. In addition to his coya and secondary wives, he had concubines, women who lived in his palace. Each Sapa Inca had hundreds of these women. They served him however he wished, even bearing his children; one ruler had seven hundred children by his concubines. The concubines' sons joined the young nobles in the House of Learning; their daughters married noblemen. The second group of Chosen Women became part of the royal "treasury," living gifts for the Sapa Inca's favorites and victorious army officers. Those in the last group led a religious life as Virgins of the Sun.

Religion played a vital part in everyday life. The Inca believed that everything was controlled by spirits and gods. If rain washed a farmer's seeds out of the ground, or lightning struck his house, it was because one of the spirits wanted to do him harm. The Inca, like other primitive peoples, used their own behavior to understand why the spirits and gods acted as they did. If people could be kind or cruel, generous and greedy, so could supernatural beings. It followed, therefore, that showing respect, offering gifts, and pleading could influence the spirits as one influences a powerful person.

The Inca worshipped *huacas,* any place or thing, natural or man-made, thought to house a spirit. A huaca might be a temple, tomb, palace, fort, battlefield, cave, spring, or lake; very powerful spirits lived in snowcapped mountains. The city of Cuzco was the Inca's largest and most sacred huaca. Plant oddities such as two ears of maize growing together or a cornstalk with a black and white ear on it were also huacas. A Sapa Inca's mummy or, indeed, anything in human form—a boulder resembling a head, twigs like bony fingers—was a huaca. People gathered at their local huacas to ask favors of the spirits and leave them gifts. At some huacas temples were built, complete with statues of the spirits and priests to care for them.

The gods were treated with still greater respect. The Inca, like all Native Americans, were polytheists, believers in many gods who controlled the forces of nature. Their chief god was Inti, the Sun, giver of light, warmth, and life itself. Inti ruled the sky by day, while Mother Moon, his sister-queen, ruled by night. Next came Ilyapa, the "Thunderer," lord of storms and hurler of lightning bolts. The Inca saw Ilyapa's shadow near the heavenly river of the Milky Way. When his sister filled her jug in the river, his lightning bolt broke it, sending the water to earth as rain. The Earthquake god lived deep in the ground. His hot breath was expelled through volcanoes, and the ground shook when he tossed in his sleep. His actions terrified the Indians, who'd weep and beg him not to destroy the world.

Priests understood the ways of the gods. Trained in divination, they could tell the future by observing certain things. Before making an important decision, an Inca might ask a priest to count a pile of small objects: maize kernels, beans, pebbles. An even count meant that the gods favored his plan; an odd count was a warning not to go ahead. Another way to read the gods' intentions was to spit coca juice onto the palm of a hand, keeping the two longest fingers extended. If the juice ran down both fingers equally, the gods were favorable; if unequally—watch out!

The priests' most important tasks, however, were supervising the gods' temples, regulating prayer, and offering sacrifices. They were assisted by the Virgins of the Sun, selected, as we've seen, from among the Chosen Women. The title Virgins of the Sun was taken seriously. These women were never allowed to see a man, not even the Sapa Inca. If one broke her vow, she and her lover

Virgins of the Sun spinning thread. Chosen for their beauty and intelligence, these young women devoted themselves to the religious life. One of their tasks was to make very fine cloth for use only by the royal family. There was a great need for this cloth, as the Sapa Inca wore a garment only once, then sent it to be burned.

were punished for crimes against Inti. Both were stripped naked, tied up, hung by the hair, and left to die of exposure. For good measure, everyone in the man's village was killed, the village destroyed, and rocks scattered so that nothing would grow there again.

Cuzco was the center of the Incan world and the holiest place in its religion. Next to Tenochtitlán, the Aztec capital, "royal Cuzco" was the largest city of the New World. It dwarfed most European cities. Cuzco and its suburbs extended thirty miles in all directions and were home to some two hundred thousand people. Like everything Inca, it was well organized. Only the Sapa Inca, his nobles, priests, and visiting chieftains lived in the city itself, along with their families and servants. Commoners lived on

28

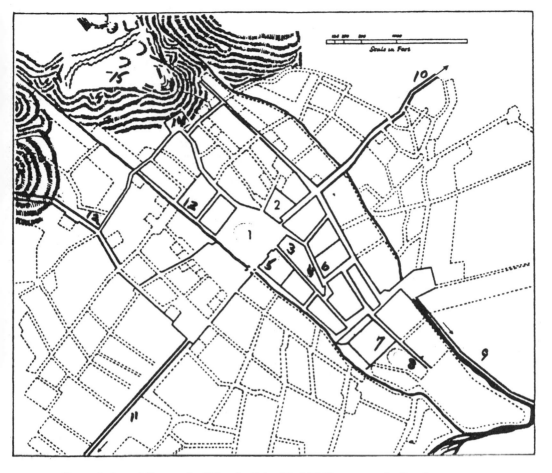

Ground plan of Cuzco, the "Navel of the World." Cuzco was the Inca's most important huaca, "holy place," and the capital of the empire.

1. Joy Square
2. Palace of Viracocha Inca
3. Palace of Huáscar
4. House of the Virgins of the Sun
5. Palace of Huayna Capac
6. Palace of Topa Inca
7. Temple of the Sun
8. Coricancha, the "Golden Enclosure"
9. Road to the southern quarter of the empire
10. Road to the eastern quarter of the empire
11. Road to the western quarter of the empire
12. Road to the northern quarter of the empire
13. House of Learning
14. Palace of Manco
15. Fortress of Sacsahumán

the outskirts in thousands of red and yellow huts. There were people from every corner of the empire, brought in as guards or because of special skills. The members of each tribe lived in their own districts and wore their own costumes. It meant death to be outside your district without permission or to wear another tribe's headdress. Hunchbacks, dwarfs, and those with harelips also had a district on the outskirts of Cuzco; the Sapa Inca kept them nearby to insure a supply of jesters for his court.

Cuzco was laid out in a huge checkerboard. Its streets were narrow and paved with stone. In addition, four main roads, one for each of the empire's "quarters," began at Joy Square, an open space of twenty acres at the city's center. Here is where the Sapa Incas' mummies were brought for festivals, and from here soldiers went off to the wars.

The House of Learning and the palaces of Sapa Incas living and dead surrounded Joy Square on three sides. These buildings, made of stone blocks, many weighing twenty tons, were marvels of engineering.

Using stone hammers and bronze chisels, quarrymen separated the huge blocks of stone from a cliff face. Because the Inca lacked the wheel and hoisting devices, the blocks were moved on wooden rollers with hundreds of men pulling on ropes. Once at the building site, the blocks were hauled on rollers up a ramp of earth built to the desired height, in much the same way as the Egyptians built their pyramids. Finally, water and sand were used to polish the blocks as smooth as glass. The blocks fit together so tightly, without mortar, that even today a knife blade can't be forced between the joints. Sometimes, however, molten silver or gold was used as mortar. Although these metals were too soft to bind heavy stones, they were worthy of the house of a god-king.

The Sapa Inca lived surrounded by the "sweat of the Sun." About seven million ounces of gold came into Cuzco every year. Once inside, it could never leave again; anyone trying to remove it died under torture. Much of the gold wound up in the royal

Inca masons at work. Without iron tools to shape stones, or cement to keep them in place, the Inca constructed great buildings and fortresses. Many examples of Inca walls may be seen in present-day Cuzco.

palaces. Every object used in a palace was made of gold or silver. Serving plates, bowls, vases, statues—all were made of precious metal. The Sapa Inca's bathtub was solid gold and fed by running water from pipes of the same metal. As if that weren't enough, the walls were gold-plated and set with jewels. Some palaces had rooms measuring 60 by 200 paces; the great hall of one palace could easily hold four thousand men.

These palaces were plain compared to the Temple of the Sun. This was the Inca holy of holies, the place where Manco Capac and Mama Ocllo first settled. The Temple of the Sun was actually a walled compound with six buildings. It was reserved for the royal family, the nobility, and the priests; commoners were kept out.

Four of the buildings were dedicated to the Moon, Stars, Thunder, and the Rainbow. A fifth building housed Inti's priests.

The main building belonged to Inti. The roof was covered with several feet of thatch to make it watertight, but mixed with the straw were thousands of solid gold "straws" that made the glittering roof visible miles away. The temple's walls, both inside and out, were covered with gold plates, each weighing from four to ten pounds. Inside, above the god's solid gold statue, was an enormous golden disk set to catch the rays of the morning sun and light up the whole shrine. Bundles of golden "firewood" were stacked in the corners. The high priest, clad in cloth of gold, offered Inti coca every morning and never approached his idol without a mouth full of the "divine herb." Two hundred Virgins of the Sun served as Inti's wives, dancing for him and offering fresh food and chicha. One was selected each night to be the Bride of the Sun and "sleep" with him; that is, lie on a blanket of woven hummingbird feathers placed on the ground near his idol.

Inti's sacred garden was next to his temple. This *coricancha,* or "golden enclosure," was one of the wonders of the world. Everything in it was gold. Golden ears of maize hung from golden

Festival of Inti, the Inca Sun god. Notice the women's foreheads. When they were babies, their mothers flattened their foreheads with boards to make them more "beautiful." Notice also the big-headed pins holding their robes closed. Such pins were often made of gold or silver.

stalks planted row upon row. A herd of golden llamas was attended by golden herdsmen. The stones of the paths were gold, as were the coca plants alongside. Golden spiders and snakes, and lizards and snails crawled about. Golden caterpillars inched along golden twigs, while golden butterflies sipped golden nectar from golden flowers. All were life-size and exact in every detail.

In front of the coricancha was an open area known as the Field of Pure Gold. A path led from it to a compound of low thatched huts. There, hundreds of young boys and girls waited their turn to be sacrificed.

Human sacrifice seems cruel to us, even insane, like the plot of some horror movie. To the Inca, it seemed perfectly sensible to keep the gods happy with gifts. Gifts were usually precious things worthy of a divinity, such as coca and the tastiest foods. Each morning the priest approaching Inti's idol with coca,

Preparing a llama for sacrifice. The priest would sacrifice this llama to the idol, hoping for some favor from the gods or that they would reveal the future to him.

33

chanted, "Eat this, Lord Sun, in recognition of the fact that we are thy children."

But human life was the finest gift of all.

Primitive peoples, not only in the New World, but in Asia, Africa, and Europe, have offered human sacrifice. The Aztecs made it the core of their religion. Each year thousands of Aztecs had their hearts cut out of their living bodies and offered to the Sun god, who was also their god of war. Thousands more were burned alive, skinned, and drowned as offerings to other gods.

The Inca were never *that* bloodthirsty. When they needed a special favor from the gods, hundreds were sacrificed. Earthquakes, crop failures, and military defeats called for sacrifices. If the Sapa Inca fell ill, or was to be crowned, human spirits were "sent" to the gods to beg their favor. People were sacrificed to the mountain gods by being left to freeze to death on their summits.

The victims were men, women, and, above all, children. The children were often boys collected in taxes from the provinces. Parents gave their babies for the public good or, if a parent were ill, in the hope that the gods would accept the young life in place of their own. Many sacrificial victims were chosen from among the Virgins of the Sun. All had to be perfect; the smallest scratch or pimple made them unworthy.

On the day of sacrifice, the victims were fed a hearty meal; mothers suckled their infants, so they shouldn't go to the gods hungry or crying. Older children were given massive doses of chicha or were drugged with coca. Then, dressed in gorgeous clothes, they were brought to a huaca or sacred place for the final act. As they danced groggily, a priest strangled them with a rope. In some cases, however, their throats were cut and their chests opened. The still-beating hearts were torn out and offered to the idol, whose face was smeared with blood from ear to ear, across the nose. Royal mummies were sometimes smeared the same way.

Terrible as human sacrifice seems to us, we should remember that the Inca thought it necessary to their well-being. Sacrificial victims were not being punished for any crime; they were being rewarded for their beauty. The killing was done as painlessly as possible and without anger or hatred. Being sacrificed was, indeed, an honor that guaranteed eternal life with the gods and thus a "favor."

The warrior, like the priest, served the Sun. The Inca idea of war differed from our own. We think that war is a disaster, a cruel waste of life and wealth. The Inca saw it as having a double benefit. It was, first, a necessity; for just as Manco Capac and Mama Ocllo spread Sun worship across the valley of Cuzco, their descendants must continue their mission, spreading it worldwide. It was their duty to conquer the world for Inti. On the other hand, war was manly. Man, they believed, is a born warrior. Fighting is as natural to him as eating. In Quecha, the Inca language, the word *auccay*—"to fight"—also means "to enjoy oneself with the enemy, to play games." The true Inca liked to "play." He hoped for war, trained for it, prayed for it. He was always a deadly foe.

The Sapa Inca had a magnificent war machine. Its peacetime strength was only the ten thousand-odd nobles who made up his bodyguard and the warriors stationed at frontier outposts. But when war threatened, the war machine would expand to between a quarter-million and three hundred thousand men. Although every able-bodied man was liable for military service, only those who could be spared from their villages were taken. When a man became a soldier, those he left behind were cared for by the community. During his absence, neighbors tilled his fields in addition to their own. His family kept everything produced, and, if he died, the community cared for them.

The Inca learned about weapons from boyhood. Bartholomé de las Casas, a Spaniard we'll meet later, left a description of their military training:

In every settlement there were instructors in the art of fighting and of manipulating weapons. They had charge of all the boys from ten to eighteen, who at certain hours

35

of the day were ordered to fight among themselves in serious or sham battles; those of the boys who proved stronger, braver, fiercer, and more skillful in the art of fighting were destined for a military career, in accordance with the orders of the king. . . . There was another method for testing the boys. . . . When they reached the age of eighteen they were aligned before a captain or a military instructor who would order a man with a club or some other weapon to "go over there and kill this man"; the man so addressed would raise his club menacingly, as if he intended to strike. If the young man, who was on trial, showed any indication of fright on his face, he was discharged and sent away, to remain a peasant all his life. . . .

The decision to go to war was taken only after careful thought. When the Sapa Inca wanted to bring another people into the empire, he sent an ambassador to speak with their leaders. The ambassador brought beautiful gifts, together with an offer they dared not refuse. In the name of the Sun, they must accept the Sapa Inca as overlord. If they accepted, he'd treat them with respect, allowing them to rule their people much as before. Refusal would bring upon them the wrath of the Son of the Sun.

Even while these talks were still going on, the Sapa Inca began what we'd call "covert operations." These were secret actions of two types: espionage and subversion. All espionage—spying—was carried out by the emperor's most trusted relatives. Like today's spies, they gathered information about enemy forces, supplies, and defenses. Subversion—undermining enemy power without violence—was equally important. Inca agents bribed the enemy's own officials and tried to isolate the enemy by bribing or threatening his allies. They also spread rumors to create fear and uncertainty. If the agents did their jobs well, the enemy was on the way to defeat well before fighting began.

Meantime, the priests made their own preparations. War to

the Inca was not just a matter of weapons and tactics. Victory and defeat, like everything else, came from the gods. To win the favor of their own gods, priests fasted, prayed, and offered sacrifices. But the enemy also had gods, and they had to be weakened. The priests did this by building a fire and dancing around it with stones on which snakes, toads, pumas, and jaguars had been painted. They danced faster and faster, as flames leaped skyward and the logs hissed and spat red cinders. As they danced, they chanted: "May it succeed! May the huacas of our enemies lose their strength!" Finally, they cut open a llama and, while it was still alive, tore out its lungs. A priest blew into a vein and noted the markings on the lungs' surface. Those markings were thought to be messages from the gods. If the markings were favorable, the army received its marching orders; if not, the war was canceled. Fighting without the gods' favor meant disaster for sure.

The Inca armies marched along the best system of roads in the world. At a time when European roads were narrow tracks, muddy and useless much of the year, the Land of the Four Quarters had ten thousand miles of all-weather roads. These formed a network linking the remotest village with Cuzco. The empire couldn't have existed without them. Roads allowed information to be carried swiftly over thousands of miles. They brought troops to resist invaders, or to crush rebels, within weeks instead of months. They also made it easy to concentrate large armies in the event of war.

Inca roads were laid out according to a simple plan. There were two great systems. The Andes road stretched along the central plateau for 3,250 miles from Ecuador to Argentina. The coast road ran for 2,520 miles along the length of Peru and deep into Chile. Over 4,000 miles of lateral roads joined the systems at key places.

The Inca road builders overcame all obstacles. They tunneled through rocks, built causeways over marshes, and bridged canyons; bridges were made of rope cables as thick as a man's

The bridge over the Apurímac River near Cuzco. The Spaniards were terrified of suspension bridges, often crossing them on hands and knees with their eyes closed. Had the Inca cut the bridges and defended the mountain passes, the invaders could never have penetrated the country so easily.

body. The coast road was twenty-four feet wide for its entire length; mountain roads were narrower, since they had to zigzag to reduce the grade on steep slopes. Roads were perfectly level and often paved with flat stones. Long stretches were bordered by trees to shade the warriors and canals to quench their thirst. Yet, apart from the army and those on official business, these magnificent roads were deserted. Ordinary people could not use them; guards were posted at the entrances to bridges and towns to see that no one traveled without official permission.

Runners called *chasquis* raced along the roads with brief, easily memorized, messages. They were not long-distance runners, for nobody could survive such exertion in the high moun-

A chasqui blows a conch-shell trumpet to call his replacement. Chasquis often carried quipus, although the key to understanding them had to be memorized. It meant death to reveal the key word to unauthorized persons.

tains. Instead, they had been trained from childhood to run short distances at top speed. Chasqui stations, each with two relief runners, were located along the roads within a mile or a mile and a half of each other. When a runner drew near, he shouted to alert the station. As he passed seconds later, his relief began to run at his side. Without slackening his pace, he repeated the message, allowing the other man to draw ahead. Then, and only then, did he stop. The chasquis were so fast that messages went the 1,250 miles from Quito and Cuzco in five days, or 250 miles a day. The Sapa Inca's generals relied on the information the messengers brought.

The army marched in ranks and under strict discipline. Soldiers could not break formation or stray from the road. Anyone who stole food from planted fields near the roadside was hung by the heels and his brains beaten out with a club. Stealing was not only wrong, but unnecessary. Every road had storehouses, or *tampus,* located a day's marching distance from one another. These were groups of stone buildings filled with food, clothing, and military supplies. A few were so large that they could supply twenty-five thousand men at a time. The roads and tampus ended, of course, at the borders of the empire. Supplies then went by llama caravan and on the backs of porters.

As soon as the enemy was sighted, the warriors dressed for battle. Each man expected both to give and to receive hard blows. To protect himself, he had a wooden shield covered with deerskin and decorated with a favorite design. On his head he wore a helmet made of chonta-palm wood, black as coal and hard as iron. His main protection, however, was a padded cotton jacket able to soften the blow of any Indian weapon. Unlike European steel armor, this jacket was lightweight and flexible, allowing one to move about freely.

The Inca approached the enemy in mass formations thousands strong. As they came within earshot, they set up an earsplitting racket; noise boosted their own courage and made the enemy

Huayna Capac in battle. The Sapa Inca, holding a shield before him and twirling his sling, leads his men in battle from atop the royal litter.

jittery. Warriors blew conch-shell trumpets and bone whistles. They shook gourd rattles and beat drums covered with human skin. Men danced wildly, whirling, jumping, shouting. They boasted of their courage and jeered the enemy as cowards. Some units bellowed a bloodcurdling rhyme:

> *We'll drink chicha from your skull*
> *From your teeth we'll make a necklace*
> *From your bones, flutes*
> *From your skin we'll make a drum*
> *And then we'll dance.*

41

INCA AND SPANIARD

"Chaya! Chaya!"—"At them! At them!"—shouted the front ranks, the missilemen, as they rushed forward. Most carried a sling, a belt of llama wool about four feet long. This was doubled around a stone the size of a hen's egg and twirled over the head before one end was released. The stone shot forward, striking with the force of a bullet. Spearmen hurled their weapons, poles with fire-hardened points. Still others loosed the *bolas,* three stone or copper balls tied to cords fastened together in the middle. When thrown at a person, the bola twirled around arms and legs, toppling the person and causing serious wounds. Last, but not least, were the archers. Although the Inca never used the bow and arrow themselves, their allies from the eastern forests could shoot a bird out of the air.

When the missilemen ran out of ammunition, the main blow was delivered face-to-face. At the general's signal, the troops broke ranks and ran toward the enemy. Once the general sent them forward, he lost control of the action. Everything now depended on personal courage, superior numbers, and close-combat weapons.

The Inca had fearsome weapons for close combat. Their favorite was a club with a star-shaped head of stone, copper, or silver. A tap with this club could easily crush a skull or shatter an arm. Equally deadly was the *macana,* a sword-shaped club made of chonta wood, and axes made of copper. The halberd was three weapons in one: a long spear together with a copper ax blade and a sharp copper hook. A halberdier could stab, hack, and snag an opponent as needed.

The battle ended when the enemy ran away or his idol was captured. Losing an idol meant that the god had abandoned his people or had been overcome by the Sun god. Either way, there was nothing to do but surrender and hope for the best.

The aftermath of battle was filled with both joy and pain. The Inca were happy, for once again Inti had given them victory, as he'd done in every major battle since 1438.

Attack on a terraced fort. While the defenders hurl down stones, the Inca, with spears, halberds, and shields, advance. The man at the right holds up an idol to rob the defenders' huacas of their power.

Yet victory never came cheaply. The wounded covered the ground, bleeding and moaning. Inca doctors came to their aid with a variety of plant medicines. Quinine was used to dress wounds and lower fever; coca was used as a painkiller. Cuts were closed with "living hooks": Large ants were made to bite through both lips of a wound; then their heads were snipped off, leaving the jaws hooked together. Doctors also operated on the skulls of men with head wounds. If one survived a blow with a war club, bone splinters might press on the brain, causing paralysis. During the operation, called trepanning, the doctor cut into the skull to remove the splinters. Many patients, of course, died. But many lived, as we know from skulls found in graves, which had healed incisions. Trepanning was used to treat George Washington's troops during the American Revolution.

The enemy soon found that Inca threats had to be taken seriously. The Inca could be very cruel, especially in avenging past insults. Yet cruelty, like everything else they did, had a purpose.

43

Not only did it allow them to release anger, it spread terror so that the *next* people would think twice about defying them. The Inca's greatest fear was of not being feared.

Their cruelty was displayed in the "trophies" they collected. The heads of enemy leaders became drinking cups. The brain was scooped from the skull and replaced with a gold cup to be filled with chicha, which was sipped through a golden tube. Soldiers made flutes of enemy arm and shin bones; necklaces of enemy teeth were popular items. But nothing was as gruesome as the "man-drums." After an enemy leader had been flayed alive, his skin was stuffed with straw and his stomach made into a drum. The thin, dangling arms were used to pound upon his belly, giving a low, hollow sound. Man-drums were displayed in Cuzco and used during festivals. The Inca found them hilarious. During festivals, they enjoyed their "music" and laughed as they shouted jokes into the drums' dead ears.

Victory was celebrated by a parade through Cuzco. With drummers and trumpeters leading the way, the army marched through the city in battle formation. All had been rewarded as they deserved: common soldiers with clothing, officers with gold and silver plates worn on the chest. The bravest, regardless of rank, received Chosen Women as wives or concubines. Next came the prisoners, their hands tied behind their backs, their wives and children trembling and weeping. The enemy chief was stretched naked on a litter, surrounded by soldiers beating drums made of his relatives and officers. Other soldiers carried enemy heads on the points of their spears. Behind the prisoners were hundreds of Chosen Women, dancing with bells on their ankles, beating tambourines, and singing. The highest nobles followed, wearing tall, feather headdresses, weighed down by golden ornaments, and chanting hymns of victory. Lesser nobles strewed flowers before the Son of the Sun. He was carried in a litter of solid gold. He sat stone-faced, riding above the throng with all the dignity of a man-god. Finally, the royal family, also in litters, brought the parade to an end.

44

A Sapa Inca receives the head of an enemy chieftain. Notice the golden plugs in his earlobes, a sign of nobility. The weight of these plugs was often so great as to stretch the earlobes to the shoulder.

The procession halted at the Temple of the Sun. Selected prisoners were taken aside and strangled in thanksgiving for victory. Their comrades, still bound, were ordered to lie with their faces touching the ground. The Sapa Inca, his nobles, and generals then walked on their necks, chanting, "My enemies I tread upon."

Not all victories, however, were celebrated in this way. Most were celebrated differently. The Sapa Inca rewarded his troops, as usual, but the defeated were treated kindly. The Inca had a genius for empire building. While other tribes were satisfied to

45

loot a neighbor and then withdraw, the Inca organized their conquests into a permanent part of the empire. Humiliating the defeated made them enemies forever. But treating them kindly won their friendship, making the Inca even more powerful.

Once a campaign ended, the Sapa Inca released his prisoners. Ordinary warriors were sent home with gifts as proof of his generosity. The defeated chiefs were not only released, they were allowed to keep their offices. Their sons were brought to Cuzco to study at the House of Learning, where, in time, they learned to think as well as act like Incas. Chiefs' daughters became Chosen Women, often marrying Inca nobles.

Yet there was no doubt about who was in charge. The conquered territory swarmed with Inca officials to "advise" the chief. They asked him, please, to allow the imperial roads to be extended into his territory. They explained why it would be good to send his craftsmen to Cuzco and his warriors to the Sapa Inca's armies; a few victims for sacrifice might also have to be sent as a gesture of friendship. Naturally, as a loyal ally, he had to place Inti above his people's other gods. He accepted all advice with a smile. There was no choice, for he knew the price to himself and his family, should he disobey. Although his children were being treated as Inca nobles, they were really hostages for his good behavior.

If a conquered tribe seemed unreliable, it was broken forever. Inca soldiers drove out entire villages and moved them to villages scattered throughout the empire. There the conquered people became tiny minorities surrounded by strangers eager to keep them in line. Their old lands were settled by *mitimaes,* Quechua for "a man sent elsewhere." These settlers were loyal Inca sent to colonize distant provinces. Although they might have loved the villages of their birth, their feelings didn't matter to the man-god in Cuzco. When he ordered them to move, they moved. It was the only time they were permitted to use the roads. Settling in the conquered country, they served as teachers to the natives and as policemen and spies for the government. No one, conqueror or conquered, could escape the power of the Son of the Sun.

46

It had taken the Inca less than a century to build one of the great empires of world history. Vigorous and wealthy, guarded by vast armies, it seemed invincible. Yet enemies stronger and crueler than they'd ever met were on the way. When they arrived, the Land of the Four Quarters would be no more, its people crushed by a tyranny none could have imagined even in nightmares.

2

THE BEARDED ONES

THE DESTRUCTION OF THE INCAN WORLD WAS LED
by Francisco Pizarro, one of the most remarkable men of a remarkable age. Pizarro was born about 1471 in the town of Trujillo
in the Spanish province of Extremadura. His father was Gonzalo
Pizarro, the One-eyed, a small landowner and army officer. His
mother was Francisca Gonzalez, a peasant girl.

Little is known about Francisco's early life, except that it
wasn't pleasant. Gonzalo was a ladies' man who sired several sons
without marrying their mothers. Francisco was his first son, but
he treated him like a stranger. He took no responsibility for the
boy's upbringing, neither supporting him nor allowing him to live
in his house. Where Francisco lived and how remains a mystery.
He may have lived with his mother's people, although one account
says she left him at the church door. According to another story,
she threw him away and a sow kept him alive with her own milk.
We'll probably never know the truth. Francisco was always tight-
lipped about his childhood, perhaps because of painful memories.

The land he grew up in didn't make his life any easier. The
Romans gave Extremadura its name, calling it *extrema et dura*,
remote and harsh. It is that, and more. Extremadura broils in

Francisco Pizarro in his full glory as governor of New Castile. At last a hidalgo, a son of someone, he wears expensive armor with a silk sash across his chest. The stick in his left hand is a baton, symbol of military authority.

summer, freezes in winter, and is poor the year round. But hardship has tempered the *extremeños*. Smiles, let alone laughter, do not come readily to them. They are an independent, stubborn breed who don't know how to admit defeat. For centuries their more adventurous sons have gone into the wider world to seek their fortunes.

During Francisco's youth, this meant becoming a soldier. There was plenty of opportunity to follow that trade in the fifteenth century. Spain and France had been at war on and off for generations. By the 1490s, just as Christopher Columbus was dreaming of reaching the East by sailing west, the war spilled over into Italy. Extremeños, among them young Pizarro, flocked to the action.

Pizarro's real education began in Italy. Education had noth-

49

ing to do with books. He never went to school or learned to read and write; he couldn't even sign his name. But Italy taught him about fighting and conquering. He served with the Spanish infantry, the terror of the battlefield. Tough, proud men, they were noted for three things: courage, cruelty, and greed. Their battle cry called upon Saint James, Spain's patron saint, to bring them victory. *"Santiago y a ellos!"* they'd shout. "Saint James and at them!" And at them they came with all the fury of a tornado. Spaniards were known to kill enemy wounded and torture prisoners until they begged for death. But *oro*, "gold," that was their true love, for gold was their passport out of poverty. With enough gold a commoner could go home, buy land, and marry a fine lady. He'd become a hidalgo—an *hijo de algo*—a "son of someone."

We can't say for certain when Francisco left for Italy or returned to Spain. What is sure is that he wasn't a "son of someone" when he returned. By then, however, everyone was talking about Columbus's discovery and how fortunes could be made across the sea. Since he had nothing to lose, in 1502 Pizarro joined the fleet Nicholas de Ovando was taking to the Caribbean. Ovando had been named governor of Hispaniola, an island shared today by Haiti and the Dominican Republic. Ovando was an extremeño, as was Pizarro's distant cousin who'd also signed up for the voyage. The cousin was nineteen-year-old Hernán Cortés. By chance the future conqueror of Mexico was to sail with the future conqueror of Peru. But this time Cortés missed the boat. While walking on a wall outside the bedroom of a girl he was courting, the wall collapsed, hurting him badly. His cousin sailed alone. It is unlikely that anyone regretted Pizarro's leaving, or that he felt homesick.

Pizarro's actions during the next seven years are unknown to us. All that is certain is that he lived in Hispaniola, stayed a bachelor, and became a respected member of the community. Yet respect isn't the same as love. After he became famous, men who'd known him at this time remembered him as tall and well built, with

Hernán Cortés, conqueror of Mexico and a distant cousin of Francisco Pizarro. They met during Pizarro's return to Spain in 1528 and probably discussed strategies of Indian warfare.

a thick black beard and eyes that seemed to bore into people, reading their innermost thoughts. He spoke little, and then softly; he seemed always to be watching people. He was a man to be trusted—when it suited his purposes. Otherwise he'd lie or accuse others of bad faith. Vengeful and suspicious, he cared nothing for others' feelings. Francisco Pizarro was a hard man to deal with, and a harder man to beat.

He might have lived out his years in Hispaniola had it not been for the explorer Alonso de Ojeda. Ojeda had wide experience in the New World. He'd commanded a ship under Columbus during his second voyage in 1493 and had visited the mainland of South America several times. There he'd found Indian villages built on stilts along the shore of a lake. Since they reminded him of Venice in Italy, he called the country Little Venice—Venezuela. Toward the end of 1509, Ojeda received permission to start a colony and search for treasure in what is now northern Colombia. Before setting out, he recruited soldiers in Hispaniola, among them Francisco Pizarro.

Ojeda found a good harbor and built a settlement called San Sebastian. But he quickly learned that a piece of paper signed in Spain meant nothing to the Indians. No sooner did his men venture outside the log-walled settlement, than they drew showers of arrows. They'd experienced Indian arrows in Hispaniola and were not worried, for most had recovered from their wounds. Imagine their surprise when they saw friends dropping to the ground thrashing and screaming, or when they swelled to twice normal size! These arrows were something special. Made of slender reeds, they had points of sharp fish scales dipped in curare, a poison made from the sap of jungle vines and snake blood.

Ojeda lost seventy men in one battle and was himself wounded in the thigh. Pulling out the arrow, he limped to his tent and called for the surgeon. The man was helpless against curare, but Ojeda had his own ideas about a treatment. He ordered the surgeon to enclose the thigh in two iron plates heated white-hot. When the surgeon hesitated, Ojeda promised to hang him for disobedience if it was the last thing he ever did. The plates were applied and burned the thigh, leaving it shriveled. Ojeda took this treatment without being held down and without crying out. The hard life of Spanish soldiers had made them scornful of pain. Crying out was unmanly and unworthy.

When Ojeda recovered, he decided to return to Hispaniola for reinforcements. Promising to return within fifty days, he left Pizarro in charge and sailed away. Although Ojeda was shipwrecked and unable to keep his promise, Pizarro now had his first command.

As days turned into weeks, the settlers became desperate. Food ran short, forcing them to live on shellfish and seaweed.

Pizarro realized that their only hope was to leave San Sebastian. Unfortunately, with sixty men and only two small boats, there wasn't room for everyone. Who should go? Who should stay behind? These were difficult questions, which Pizarro decided to let time answer for him. He'd wait for starvation, disease, and arrows to do their work, then jam the survivors into the boats.

His plan worked. Within six months only enough men remained alive to fill the boats. After killing their last horses and salting the meat for the voyage, they set a course for Hispaniola. But one of the boats sank in the rough sea, forcing Pizarro to take the survivors aboard his own vessel and return to the coast. The men were fast losing hope when, as if by a miracle, two vessels were sighted. Martin de Enciso, Ojeda's partner, arrived with one hundred fifty men and fresh supplies. So much time had passed since the expedition had left Hispaniola that Enciso, fearing trouble, had set out with a relief party. It was Pizarro's good luck to be rescued in the nick of time.

Although Pizarro wanted to go on to Hispaniola, Enciso insisted that they return to San Sebastian. A lot of money had gone into the expedition and he wasn't going to have it wasted because of a few quitters. After more storms at sea, they reached the abandoned settlement, only to find it had been destroyed by the Indians, who still had plenty of poisoned arrows. Clearly, the Spaniards had to find another place for their colony. But where? Pizarro knew little about the country; Enciso, a lawyer, knew nothing. But just when things seemed blackest, they were saved by someone named Balboa, who should never have been on the expedition.

Vasco Nuñez de Balboa was an extremeño who'd come to Hispaniola to make his fortune in farming. Unfortunately, he wasn't a good farmer and soon went broke. People to whom he owed money hounded him day and night, threatening to put him into jail if he didn't pay up. Desperate for a way out of his troubles, he hid in one of the barrels being loaded onto Enciso's ship, emerging when the ship was well out to sea. Enciso was furious. For a while he threatened to put Balboa ashore on one of the Caribbean islands. This was no kindness, for Spanish sea captains frequently used stowaways and criminals as guinea pigs. They'd leave them on islands inhabited by strange Indians. Some of these Indians were Caribs, from which we get the name Caribbean. We also get the name "cannibal" from this name. If a castaway was still alive when a ship returned, the captain knew the Indians were friendly and the island safe. If the castaway had disappeared— well, one less criminal to hang.

Enciso allowed Balboa to stay aboard, surely the smartest thing he'd ever done. Balboa had visited this coast before and knew a place to the south where food was plentiful and the Indians had no curare. Within a few days, the expedition had landed at the mouth of the Darien River in Panama, where they built Santa Maria de la Antigua, the first European settlement on the mainland of the New World. There the settlers elected Balboa their leader and hustled Enciso aboard a ship bound for Hispaniola.

Balboa was no ordinary adventurer. An intelligent man, he realized that, if there was gold in the area, the Indians would know where to find it. He became friendly with the chief of a local tribe, marrying one of his daughters. The tribe gave the Spaniards all the food they wanted, in return for which the Spanish helped them fight their enemies. At the end of the war, the chief held a victory celebration. To show his gratitude, he gave Balboa several large pieces of gold.

Even while the gold was being weighed, the Spaniards began quarreling about their shares. Suddenly the chief's son knocked the scales from their hands and scolded them for their greed. "What is the matter, you Christian men, that you so greatly value so small an amount of gold more than your own peace. . . . If it is for gold that you leave your homeland to disturb other people, I will show you a region flowing with gold, where you may satisfy your ravening appetites." Then, pointing to mountains in the

54

south, he said: "When you are passing over these mountains
. . . you shall see another sea, where they sail in ships big as yours,
using both sails and oars as you do, although the men be naked
as we are."

The Spaniards' mouths dropped open and their eyes blazed.
They'd never expected this! Columbus had sailed west across the
Atlantic to reach India, only to have the New World block his way.
Yet, he believed, India was very close, if only he could get around
the barrier. And now Indians were talking about a sea and a golden
land just over a nearby mountain range. Surely that sea was the
Atlantic and the golden land India! Already they pictured them-
selves as hidalgos, loaded down with the treasures of the East.

Balboa set out to find "India" on September 1, 1513, with one
hundred ninety Spaniards, hundreds of Indian porters, and a pack
of dogs. These dogs, called bloodhounds, were not the gentle,
floppy-eared creatures we know today. They were more like huge
pit bull dogs trained to rip out a man's throat on command.
Leoncito, "Little Lion," Balboa's favorite, was so ferocious that
the Spaniards themselves kept their distance. Indians who challenged the expedition discovered their error too late. Forty were
captured and torn apart, alive, for the Spaniards' amusement.

The distance to be covered was only forty-five miles, and the
mountains were less than a thousand feet high. This was not a long
journey. Yet, for all the Spaniards knew, they could have been on
another planet. The jungle was a strange world, alive with beauty
and menace. Butterflies crowded around mud puddles in the
clearings, sipping the water; when disturbed, they rose at once,
creating innumerable pinpoints of blue as their wings caught the
sunlight. Parrots with streaming tails of red and green scolded in
the treetops. Hummingbirds flashed by, winged jewels of green
and gold. Monkeys chattered as they leaped from branch to
branch. Jaguars moved silently, shadowlike, stalking their next
meal. Alligators lay motionless along the riverbanks, like mud-
covered logs, waiting for a meal to come to them.

INCA AND SPANIARD

The Spaniards' route passed through jungle so thick that days passed without their seeing the sky. Worse than the jungle were the rivers and swamps. To cross these, they had to strip naked and carry their gear over their heads. A crossing could take hours, with slime oozing through their toes and gnats, whose bites felt like hot coals, buzzing about their heads. Cloudbursts and damp, suffocating heat tormented them, causing itchy skin rashes. Yet they kept going; they'd have stormed hell for a sackful of gold.

On September 25 they stood at the base of one of the peaks the chief's son had pointed out. Commanding the others to remain below, Balboa climbed to the top alone. What he saw took his breath away. In the distance, going on it seemed forever, was a magnificent ocean. Balboa fell to his knees and, raising his hands to heaven, thanked God for making him the first European to see El Mar del Sur, the "South Sea." Recovering, he signaled his men to join him. After setting up a wooden cross, he sent Pizarro with a patrol to find a trail to the coast. Pizarro, who'd become his friend, was one of his chief captains.

The expedition reached the coast a few days later. The Spaniards, clad in full armor, stood there with the wind in their faces and the roar of the surf in their ears. As waves rushed over the sandy beach, Balboa, with a sword in one hand and a Spanish flag in the other, waded in up to the waist. "Long live the mighty and powerful kings of Castile,"* he cried. "In their name I take possession of these seas and regions; and if any prince, be he Christian or infidel, claims any right to these, I am ready to contradict him, and to defend them." Without knowing the extent of the South Sea, or about the people who lived along its shores, he'd taken possession of everything for his king.

---

*Spain was made up of two large kingdoms, Castile and Aragon, plus several smaller ones. The marriage of Isabella of Castile and Ferdinand of Aragon in 1469 united nearly the whole country under the "Catholic Kings." Grenada, a Moorish, or Muslim, kingdom was conquered in 1492, the same year Columbus sailed for India.

The Spaniards remained on the coast for several months, exploring and visiting the local tribes. By using sign language and some Indian words they knew, they learned that there was, indeed, a rich land far to the south. The Indians had no idea what that land was called, only that it was ruled by "kings of gold." None had ever seen any of their people, but they knew others who had. They also drew an outline in the sand of an animal found in this land. The Spaniards, who'd never seen a llama, called it a "long-haired deer." Best of all, the Indians gave them gifts of gold. It hadn't taken them long to realize that their visitors could never get enough of the yellow metal.

In the meantime, Martin de Enciso had returned to Spain with his tale of how Balboa had mistreated him. He had powerful friends at court, and these persuaded King Ferdinand to appoint Pedro Arias de Avila as governor of the colony. The governor, known simply as Pedrarias, sailed with fifteen hundred men, scores of secretaries and assistants, and a bishop to minister to the colonists' spiritual needs. Arriving at Santa Maria de la Antigua in June 1514, he found Balboa, back from the South Sea, full of plans for exploration and conquest. Jealous of Balboa's discoveries and resenting his influence in the colony, Pedrarias decided to get rid of him—permanently.

While the governor laid his plans, he allowed Balboa to continue his explorations. Balboa built two brigantines, light vessels that were taken through the jungle in sections and assembled on the shore of the South Sea. Sailing in these, Balboa discovered the Pearl Islands, whose offshore waters swarmed with pearl-bearing clams, and explored Panama's west coast. One day in 1517, as he was preparing to search for the golden lands to the south, he received an order to report to the governor. No sooner did he arrive, than Francisco Pizarro met him with an armed guard and placed him under arrest. If there was something to be gained for himself, Pizarro would betray anyone.

Balboa and three of his officers were tried on trumped-up

charges of treason and sentenced to death. It was said that Pizarro commanded the guards during the execution. Perhaps he did, but there is no proof either way. He certainly witnessed the last moments of the condemned. They were brought out of jail with their hands tied behind their backs. Mounting a raised platform, they saw the assembled townsmen looking up at them, many with tears running down their cheeks. Then they saw the executioner, his arms bare, his face covered with a black mask. Each in turn kneeled in front of a bloodstained wooden block and the executioner cut off his head with a single stroke of an ax. The heads were displayed on poles set up in the public square and the bodies tossed to the vultures.

With the death of his "friend," Pizarro vanishes from history for another seven years. All that is known is that he was granted some farmland when Pedrarias founded Panama City on the coast of the South Sea in 1519. Along with the land went Indian slaves, who produced enough to support themselves and their master. Although he wasn't wealthy, Pizarro lived comfortably on the labor of others. Even if he'd wanted to continue Balboa's explorations, he couldn't have moved without the governor's permission.

Pedrarias, however, wasn't interested in southern voyages. Stories of kingdoms of gold, he insisted, were just that: stories made up by Indians and exaggerated by gold-crazy settlers. The gold Balboa had brought back wasn't enough to justify sending out expensive expeditions. Like so many others, he believed the South Sea was connected to the Atlantic by a strait, or narrow body of water, cutting across Central America. We know that there was no such strait then; an artificial strait, the Panama Canal, was opened only in 1914.

Pedrarias sent expeditions westward and northward to find the nonexistent strait. On the way his men conquered western Panama and the area that is now Costa Rica and Nicaragua. They pushed as far as Honduras, where, in 1522, they met other Spaniards moving southward.

The year 1522 was a critical one. Pizarro's cousin, Hernán Cortés, had made good after all. Recovering from his injuries, he'd settled in Hispaniola and become a prosperous landowner. Attracted by rumors of a powerful kingdom on the mainland, he discovered the Aztec empire in Mexico in 1519. Within three years, he'd defeated the Aztecs and was sending troops to conquer as far south as Honduras. Also, at that very moment, Ferdinand Magellan's expedition returned to Spain after a three-year voyage. Magellan had done the "impossible." Sailing westward across the Atlantic, he'd discovered the Strait of Magellan at the southern tip of South America and entered the South Sea. He found the sea so calm at first that he named it El Mar Pacifico, the "Peaceful Ocean." The name stuck, and from then on it was called the Pacific. Although Magellan died during the voyage, the survivors' return proved that the earth was round.

The news of Cortés and Magellan landed like a bombshell among the Spanish settlers. If Cortés could strike it rich in Mexico, then others might do so elsewhere. And Mexico was not India. Indeed, as Magellan's voyage proved, Panama was nowhere near India, but part of an entirely New World. Those stories about a golden king to the south might be true after all.

Pedrarias gave permission to Pascal de Andagoya, a soldier in the colony, to follow up Balboa's explorations. Setting sail toward the end of 1522, Andagoya landed on the coast of Colombia near the mouth of the Biru River. There he met Indians wearing golden ornaments, which they gladly exchanged for some iron hatchets. When asked in sign language where the gold came from, they waved and cried "Biru." The Spaniards pronounced it "Peru." From then on, Peru was their name for the mysterious land of gold.

Andagoya's return stirred old memories in Francisco Pizarro. He was now past fifty, old by the standards of the day, but as fit as anyone half his age. He'd spent twenty years in the New World and, it seemed, he would die there. But the sight of Andagoya's

Diego de Almagro as imagined by a sixteenth-century artist.

gold brought him to one of the most important decisions in the history of discovery. He decided to continue where Balboa had left off.

It so happened that his neighbor was Diego de Almagro, who, like himself, was in his fifties, illiterate, and born out of wedlock. But that's where the similarity ended. Where Pizarro was tall and soft-spoken, Almagro was short and outspoken. He had an explosive temper and used such foul language that, supposedly, his voice shriveled the leaves in the trees.

Pizarro told Almagro about his adventures with Balboa and he, too, was bitten by the gold bug. They went to Father Hernando de Luque, a wealthy priest and friend of the governor's. The three formed a partnership to find the golden land and conquer it. Each had a special role to play in the scheme. Pizarro would do the finding and conquering. Almagro would be the middleman, remaining in Panama to gather supplies and reinforcements. Father Luque would deal with the governor and raise money from friendly merchants.

Nothing could have happened without Father Luque. Governor Pedrarias was a jealous man, not likely to permit anything he couldn't control or take credit for. Luque persuaded him to allow the expedition to go ahead in return for a twenty-five-percent share of the profits. Pedrarias agreed. After all, he had nothing to lose and everything to gain. If the scheme failed, the partners would take the loss; if it succeeded, he'd become rich without doing any work or suffering any hardship.

Two years passed before the expedition was ready to sail. Finally, on November 14, 1524, Pizarro raised anchor and slipped out of the harbor of Panama. On board were one hundred twelve Spaniards and several Indians trained as interpreters. His vessel was one of the brigantines built by Balboa, a leaky tub that had lain unmasted since the explorer's death. Almagro was to follow later with reinforcements and supplies. They'd agreed that Pizarro would leave signs for him—wooden crosses, piles of stones, blazes on trees—wherever he landed along the coast.

Sixteenth-century sea voyages were unpleasant under the best conditions. Even the galleons, those floating fortresses with dozens of cannon, had few comforts. Shipboard life was cramped, damp, dirty, and noisy. Space belowdecks was so limited that crewmen scarcely had room to move around. Since there were no bunks, they slept on the bare wooden deck. Sleeping quarters were dark and stuffy, swarming with vermin large and small. Men were forever slapping roaches and picking lice out of the seams of their clothes. Toilet facilities were nasty. Seats were fastened to overhangs near the ship's bows, near the anchor chains. Using the toilet usually meant having a saltwater bath as well; a tarred piece of rope used by all served in place of toilet paper. Food was salt beef tough as shoe leather, yellowish water, and wormy biscuit hard as brick. Really hungry men ate anything; Magellan's crews caught rats, said to taste like "chicken"—provided you didn't look at their faces. Everyone stank, since fresh water was too precious to be used for washing. But after a while the odor became unnoticeable, for everyone stank alike.

Shipboard life had already weakened Pizarro's men when they landed near the mouth of the Biru River. No Indians were to be seen this time, let alone nuggets of gold. Stretching before them was a muddy river bordered by jungle. In order to move inland, they had to cut their way through thick vines and creepers. Every step was an ordeal, as the mud sucked at their rotting boots. It was like opening one door only to be confronted by another, and another, leading nowhere. Every path ended at a swamp or in a thicker forest. After a week in this green hell, Pizarro ordered his men back to the ship.

Yet their troubles had only just begun. For ten days they sailed through a storm such as none of them had ever seen before. The wind howled without letup. Lightning bolts flashed across the black sky and rain fell in sheets. The ship heaved and tossed, bounced and rolled, in the waves. Men lay belowdecks, seasick and vomiting.

The storm passed, and they sailed along the coast, landing now and then to probe inland. It was always the same: jungle, dampness, heat, hunger. Rations were down to two ears of corn per man per day when Pizarro decided to send the vessel to the Pearl Islands to search for supplies; he dared not send it back to Panama for fear that Pedrarias would order him to return. The vessel was to return within two weeks. Yet two weeks feels like forever to men with empty stomachs.

In the meantime, Pizarro made camp at a little harbor on the Colombian coast. The men named it Puerto de la Hambre, "Hungry Harbor." The two weeks passed, then four weeks, without a sign of the vessel. Desperate for food, Pizarro's crew ate anything they could find. Except for an occasional snake or small animal taken in the jungle, they lived on seaweed, shellfish, and roots. But they were fighters, not botanists, and couldn't tell a poisonous root from a potato. Men died painfully every day.

Toward the end of the sixth week, a scouting party stumbled upon a small village in a clearing. Every man who could walk took his sword and followed Pizarro to the clearing. The moment the Indians saw these bearded scarecrows, they fled in terror. The Spaniards broke into the huts and found some corn, which they gulped down like famished wolves.

After a while, the Indians' curiosity got the best of them. Timidly they returned and began to speak to one of Pizarro's Indian interpreters. Yet their surprise in meeting these strangers was nothing compared to the Spaniards'. For the Indians, naked as they were, wore shiny yellow ornaments. True, the ornaments were poorly made, but they were of gold. One question followed another, and Pizarro soon had the information he needed. To the south lay a powerful kingdom where gold was plentiful. On the march back to Hungry Harbor, Pizarro met a messenger who reported that the relief ship had arrived. With bellies full and hopes raised, they put to sea once again.

Landing at various places along the coast, they met other Indians. These, however, were neither curious nor friendly. As soon as the Spaniards came ashore, the Indians abandoned their villages, leaving everything behind. In one village "everything" included human arms and legs stewing in a pot. Sometimes the Indians attacked. Once Pizarro's men were ambushed by painted warriors shooting arrows tipped with sharp bones. Although the arrows weren't poisoned, they killed five Spaniards and wounded seventeen. Pizarro himself was wounded seven times and barely escaped with his life. The Spaniards fought with reckless courage that day, imagining themselves, perhaps, in the cannibals' cooking pots. With their food nearly gone once again, Pizarro decided to return to Panama.

During a stopover along the coast, he met Almagro, who'd

been searching for him. Almagro had his own stories to tell. He'd also fought Indians, losing an eye during one battle. Yet he cared less about that eye than about what he'd seen with the other. He, too, had found Indians with gold and heard stories about the golden kingdom to the south.

Governor Pedrarias wasn't impressed. The golden kingdom was always "to the south," but no one seemed able to find it. All he knew was that men had died and supplies had been wasted for a few pieces of gold. He was threatening to cancel further expeditions when Father Luque saved the day. Luque persuaded him to allow the partners to try one more time. Pedrarias, sure that they'd fail, gave up all claims to future profits for a thousand gold pesos. This proved to be one of the worst bargains ever made. If he'd had more faith, he might have become as rich as some European kings.

On March 10, 1526, the partners met in Father Luque's house. On a table lay a document written on parchment. The document was a contract explaining each man's rights and obligations. It began with the words: "In the Name of the most Holy Trinity, Father, Son and Holy Ghost, three Persons and only one true God, and of Our Lady the Most Holy Virgin, we form this company . . . to discover and conquer the lands and provinces of those kingdoms called Peru." It then set out in detail how the loot would be divided. Each partner would receive exactly one third of the peoples, lands, and treasures of Peru. After the contract was read aloud, Luque signed, followed by witnesses who signed for his illiterate partners, who drew the sign of the cross next to their names. Without knowing anything of the people, government, or religion of Peru, they'd already conquered it, on paper, and divided it among themselves.

The contract's religious language had a double purpose. It bound the partners to keep their pledge or be branded liars in the sight of God. Equally important, it showed that the conquest would not only be for loot, but in the name of religion. Greed and

64

God were a powerful combination. The sixteenth-century Spaniard believed that the Indians were pagans and that their souls would forever burn in hell unless they became Christians. The *conquistadores,* "conquerors," saw themselves as God's servants. It was their duty to bring the natives to the true faith, even if that meant killing their bodies to save their souls. Not for a moment did they doubt their right to shed blood for a "higher" cause.

Pizarro, however, only pretended to believe in such an ideal. He once told a priest who urged him to consider religion and not gold in his dealings with the Indians: "I have not come for any such reasons. I have come to take away from them their gold."

Late in November 1526, two ships headed south from Panama. On board were one hundred sixty conquistadores and a few horses. Although Pizarro and Almagro were in command, they left the ships' handling to Bartholomew Ruiz, an experienced navigator. Had it not been for him, they would surely have failed to discover Peru.

Instead of hugging the coast as Pizarro had done, Ruiz made for the open ocean. The winds were more favorable out there, and the ships moved swiftly. Upon reaching the mouth of the San Juan River in Colombia, they landed. There the commanders decided to separate. Almagro returned to Panama for reinforcements, while Ruiz scouted the waters to the south. Pizarro began to search for gold.

The march inland was a carbon copy of earlier marches. Once the Spaniards left the coast, they faced nature at its most unforgiving. In addition to heat and mud, they were tormented by mosquitoes; ticks burrowed under their skin; leeches sucked their blood. Painted Indians, invisible in the brush, shot arrows at the weary men. After nearly three months of this, Pizarro returned to the coast. A few days later, Ruiz returned.

The navigator had a fantastic story to tell. He'd continued southward along the coast of present-day Ecuador. As his ship neared the equator, a lookout began to shout. There, to the south, a white sail billowed. A half hour later, the sail was seen to be attached to a raft. But what a raft! It was a balsa, an Indian craft made of giant tree trunks lashed together with ropes. The stern, or rear section, had a large cabin with a thatched roof.

Ruiz drew alongside and, for the first time, Europeans stood face to face with subjects of the Sapa Inca. The Indians showed curiosity rather than fear, and through sign language invited the sailors to come aboard. The balsa was filled with beautiful things. The Spaniards marveled at gold cups, mirrors of polished silver, and gold and silver ornaments studded with emeralds. There were piles of delicate cloths dyed in bright colors and embroidered with figures of birds, fish, and flowers.

Ruiz learned that the vessel was a trader from the port of Tumbes, some three hundred miles farther south. Was there gold in Tumbes? The Indians laughed and gestured that there was more gold there than wood in their two vessels combined. Ruiz smiled politely, hiding his excitement. Before parting company, he persuaded three Indians to transfer to his ship; they would be well treated and taught the Spanish language. One of them was given the name Felipillo, "Little Philip," and became the conquistadores' first Inca "tongue," or interpreter.

Pizarro's men had barely gotten over their excitement at Ruiz's story when Almagro arrived. He also had good news. His ship was loaded with supplies and brought eighty more volunteers. Moreover, Pedrarias had been replaced as governor by Pedro de los Rios, an honest, fair-minded person.

Once again the expedition put to sea. Along the coast they saw signs of a large population. These people were not jungle savages, who fled at the approach of strangers, but confident, possibly civilized, people. But unlike Ruiz's traders, they were unfriendly. Indians came out in canoes to threaten the strangers. Warriors marched along the shore, keeping an eye on the ships. Pizarro finally had enough of threats. Nearing a big settlement, he decided to test the Indians' courage. He landed with a small party of horsemen, daring the Indians to attack. That was a mistake. Within minutes, the Spaniards were surrounded by thousands of warriors.

"Santiago y a ellos!" the Spaniards cried as they charged. But each time they tried to break free, they were stopped by a storm of arrows and stones. Just when it seemed that all was lost, they were saved by a freak accident. Some Spaniards were preparing to charge, when a horse stumbled, tossing its rider from the saddle. Horses were unknown in the New World until the arrival of the Spaniards. The South American Indans, like their Aztec cousins, at first thought horse and rider were one animal. When the Spaniard fell, and man and horse ran in separate directions, the Indians thought the animal had broken apart. They were so surprised that they backed away, allowing the Spaniards to reach their ships.

That night the leaders held a council of war. Clearly, if this skirmish was a sample of what lay ahead, they'd need more than a handful of men. Once again, Almagro would have to return to Panama for supplies and reinforcements. Once again, Pizarro would have to await his return in some godforsaken spot.

The ships sailed to Gallo Island—Isle of the Cock—off the Ecuadorian coast. After taking on water, Almagro put to sea, bound for Panama. By then, however, most of Pizarro's men were discouraged and eager to get away. They resented Pizarro, openly saying that he wouldn't be satisfied until he'd sent them all to their graves. One sailor expressed their feelings in a message hidden in a ball of raw cotton sent aboard Almagro's ship as a gift for the governor's wife. It was a poem in which Almagro was depicted as a herdsman gathering sheep for the butcher Pizarro to slaughter:

> *Look out, Mister Governor,*
> *For the drover while he's near;*
> *Since he goes home to get the sheep,*
> *For the butcher who stays here.*

Soon afterward, Pizarro put the loudest complainers aboard the other ship and sent them back to Panama as well. Now they were alone, stranded on the Isle of the Cock until—until when?

The moment Governor Rios read the poem, he decided to end the expedition. Two ships commanded by an officer named Tafur were sent to bring everyone back to Panama. But two can play the secret-message game. Almagro had asked one of Tafur's crewmen to take a message to Pizarro. In it he urged his partner to ignore Rios's order, noting that to return now would mean that their sufferings had been for nothing. He and Luque were working to gather reinforcements and would send them as soon as possible. Meantime, Pizarro must hold out at all costs.

When Tafur arrived, he found a band of half-drowned scarecrows. It was the wet season and rain fell without letup. Pizarro and his men were nearly naked, their clothes hanging on them in sodden tatters. Many lay curled up, shaking with the chills of malaria. For weeks they'd eaten nothing but shellfish found along the shore and, for a treat, boiled pieces of leather belts. No wonder most welcomed the governor's order to abandon this pesthole.

But while Pizarro's men cheered, their commander sat on a rock, brooding with his head between his hands. Nothing he might do seemed right. By disobeying the governor's order, he'd open himself to charges of treason—and Balboa had died for less. Deep down he *knew* he was right. To give up now meant betraying himself in his own eyes. The idea of self-betrayal was worse than death. At that moment something clicked inside Francisco Pizarro. He rose above his troubles to become a true leader.

Pizarro walked to the beach where boats waited to take his men to the ships offshore. Silently he stood before the men, looking into their eyes. Drawing his sword, he traced a line in the sand from east to west. "Friends and comrades," he said, pointing the blade to the south. "This is the way to toil, hunger, nakedness, drenching storms, aye, perhaps death, though the death worthy of soldiers of the King of Castile and of the Holy Church. This is the way to Peru; the way to glory and riches." Pausing, he pointed to the north and hissed in contempt: "There lies Panama, desertion, and poverty. Choose, each man, which side of this line becomes a good Castilian." With that he stepped across the line to the south.

All but thirteen turned away, averting their eyes from Pizarro and from one another. Tafur shrugged his shoulders, amazed at such insanity. But since even lunatics must eat, he left some food and set sail for Panama.

Pizarro, the thirteen, and the three Indians from the balsa were alone. Yet their courage didn't stop the rains, or end their loneliness. Before long, the food ran out and they faced starvation once again. Determined not to leave their bones on the Isle of the Cock, they built a raft and paddled the seventy-five miles to another island, Gorgona.

Life was a bit easier on Gorgona. There was small game, and their Indians taught them to lay traps. Shellfish were plentiful, as was fresh water from streams. To keep up their spirits, Pizarro told them how rich they'd be when their luck changed, as change it must. Every morning they prayed; every evening they sang hymns. All day, every day, for seven months, they looked northward, hoping to see a sail.

Then it happened. A ship appeared, but it would have passed had they not fired a gun. Bartholomew Ruiz, who'd returned with Tafur in order to help the partners, was in command. Ruiz explained that the governor had been so angry with Pizarro that he'd refused to send any aid. Luckily, Almagro and Luque had changed his mind—up to a point. He'd allowed them to send a supply vessel, but no reinforcements. Pizarro could sail wherever he wished, but if he wasn't in Panama at the end of six months, he'd be sorry.

That's all Pizarro wanted to hear. Within three weeks he'd crossed the equator and dropped anchor in Tumbes harbor. Even from the distance Tumbes seemed a large, prosperous place surrounded by green fields. It stood on the border of the Land of the Four Quarters, the most important of its northern coastal cities. In the mountains beyond lay Quito, conquered a few years earlier by Huayna Capac, the Young Lord Rich in Virtues. Pizarro had discovered Peru.

A squadron of balsas filled with warriors met the ship as it entered the harbor. Felipillo hailed them, saying the Spaniards came in peace. The balsas drew alongside and Indians climbed aboard to stare at the whiteskins. Soon another raft arrived with gifts of fish, fruit, and llamas. So, Pizarro thought, the "long-haired deer" he'd heard about in Panama years before were real after all.

One of the rafts was commanded by an Inca nobleman. His clothes were of fine cloth; heavy gold disks had stretched his earlobes to his shoulders. *"Orejon,"* the Spaniards whispered among themselves. And from then on they called Inca nobles *orejones,* "big ears."

Pizarro welcomed the big ears, showed him around the ship, and gave him a meal of Spanish food. He enjoyed the meal, particularly the wine, which he said was better than chicha. When he asked where the Spaniards were from, Pizarro said that they served the greatest ruler on earth. They'd come from across a distant sea to teach about the one true God. The big ears listened silently. He was too polite to contradict his host after such a nice meal. But he knew that his Sapa Inca ruled the civilized world and that there were many gods. As he said good-bye, he invited the strangers to visit Tumbes.

Next day, Pizarro sent a soldier named Alonso de Molina and a black sailor ashore with some pigs and chickens for the local chief. Natives rushed from their homes to see these wonderful beings. Each time a pig oinked or a cock crowed, they burst out laughing. But the men themselves were the most fascinating curiosities. People crowded around Molina, stroking and tugging at his beard; the natives, with little facial hair, didn't think it possible

Belgian artist Théodore de Bry drew Pizarro's landing at Tumbes in his *India Occidentalis,* "West Indies," published between 1590 and 1634. The picture shows three actions taking place at once: men furling sails in preparation for landing, soldiers setting out for shore, and meeting the Indians. The Inca, of course, wore ponchos, not loincloths. Ponchos were large rectangles of cloth with a hole cut out for the head. It is unlikely that all the Indians Pizarro met had the bodies of weight lifters.

to grow such a bush. Some partially undressed him to see if he was white all over. The black sailor was an even greater puzzle. Plainly, one so black must be dirty, and the natives tried to wash him clean. The women were especially curious. Using sign language, they promised that, if the men stayed, they could marry the prettiest girls in town.

INCA AND SPANIARD

When the two men returned to their ship, they couldn't stop talking about what they'd seen. There were many beautiful women in Tumbes. And lots of gold: golden necklaces, golden bracelets, golden drinking vessels.

Their report was so wild that Pizarro sent Pedro de Candia, his chief gunner, to see what was going on. When Candia stepped ashore next day, he seemed like a god of war come from the sky. Tall and bearded, he glistened in armor from head to toe. In his right hand he held a sword whose blade flashed like lightning; over his shoulder he carried a harquebus, an early version of the musket. Felipillo had told the natives that the bearded ones used "thunder sticks" that sped invisible stones through clouds of smoke. When the Indians asked for a demonstration, Candia aimed at a wooden board and pulled the trigger. The gun spoke with a voice of thunder and a tongue of flame, shattering the board to splinters. The Indians fell on the ground and hid their faces. That thunder stick was a huaca, the home of death-dealing spirits.

Recovering from their shock, they took Candia on a tour of Tumbes. Molina and the sailor, Candia discovered, had actually seen very little. He saw temples with gold-plated walls and a miniature coricancha, complete with golden flowers and butterflies. Through sign language he learned that Tumbes was modest, compared to a place called Cuzco. There, their lord, the Sapa Inca, Son of the Sun, had his capital. As usual, it lay "far to the south," nestled amid snowcapped mountains.

Pizarro was both happy and annoyed when he heard Candia's report. He was happy because he'd found the treasure house of the New World, richer by far than Mexico. He was annoyed because he couldn't put his hands on the treasure right away. He decided to do the next best thing. He'd continue the voyage, feigning friendship toward the Indians and no interest in their gold. His men mustn't steal gold, or even accept it as gifts. But they would remember what they'd seen and where. When the time came, they'd return with an army. Then all would be theirs.

Leaving Tumbes, they continued their journey. Southward, always southward, they sailed. To their right the blue Pacific stretched to the ends of the earth. To their left they saw brown desert with a wall of mountains looming behind. Here and there, they passed villages where mountain streams had turned valleys green. Row upon row of terraces marched up the mountainsides, green with corps. The Spaniards were no strangers to agricultural terraces, or *andenes,* and they called these mountains the Andes. When they'd seen enough, they turned back. After a stopover at Tumbes, where Alonso de Molina and another man decided to stay, Pizarro's ship reached Panama toward the end of 1527. They'd been away, not six months but eighteen, and had been given up for dead.

At about this time, Huayna Capac was strolling in the gardens of his palace at Tumibamba near Quito. For the past sixteen years, this had been his favorite spot in the whole world. During his conquest of Ecuador, he'd fallen in love with Tocto Coca, "Tender Coca," the daughter of the king of Quito. He loved her so deeply that, when she died, he had no desire to live in his own capital. He chose to live out his days in her native land, close to her spirit. Quito became a kind of second capital, where the Sapa Inca stationed the finest units of his army.

On this day a breathless chasqui dropped to the ground before his lord. The chasqui had crossed the mountains to report a strange occurrence. A "house in the sea," he explained with downcast eyes, had been seen drifting along the coast. When it stopped at Tumbes, it was found to contain unknown beings. These *Suncasapa,* "Bearded Ones," had white skins, wore silver clothes, and were masters of lightning and thunder. Huayna Capac was unable to speak when he heard this; he went to his quarters, where he stayed alone until evening. In the days that followed, chasquis brought similar reports from other cities along the coast. Huayna Capac was terrified. "Get out! Get out!" he'd cry, only to have the messengers return and repeat their stories over and over.

His mind was haunted by memories of other strange events. About ten years before, the land had been torn by violent earthquakes that split the ground and caused mountains to collapse. Mama Cocha, the sea to the west, had also become angry, hurling huge waves against the shore. Although these were natural occurrences, the Inca saw them as omens, warnings from the gods about future disasters.

Another omen had appeared in the sky. The moon was surrounded by three colored rings: the first, bloodred; the second, greenish black; the third, white and smoky. A holy man "read" their meaning to Huayna Capac in a voice choked with tears:

Oh, my only lord, know you that your mother the Moon, who is always merciful, warns you that the great Pachacamac,* creator and support of the entire universe, threatens your family and your Empire with great trials that he will soon visit upon you. For this first blood-colored ring, surrounding your mother, means that a very cruel war will break out among your descendants, after you will have departed to rest beside your father the Sun; your royal blood will be shed in such streams that after a few years nothing will remain of it. The black ring threatens your religion, your laws and the Empire, which will not survive these wars and the death of your people; and all you have done, and all your ancestors have done, will vanish in smoke, as is shown by the third ring.

Huayna Capac was terrified at these omens, but after a while settled down when nothing happened.

---

*Known as Pachacamac to the coastal peoples and Viracocha to the mountain dwellers, he was the Lord of Beginnings, creator of the world and everything in it, including the Sun.

The coming of the Bearded Ones rekindled Huayna Capac's fears. Who were they? Were they gods or the messengers of gods? What did they want? He didn't know, and not knowing tormented him.

He found the answers in late 1526 or early 1527. After the Bearded Ones disappeared up the coast in their sea-house, an epidemic broke out in the Land of the Four Quarters. It may have been typhus, a disease marked by high fever and a dark red rash. But whatever it was, it was new to the Indians. The Spaniards had introduced several deadly diseases to the Americas: typhus, smallpox, scarlet fever, measles, bubonic plague. Wherever they went, they carried these diseases in their bodies, clothes, and ships. Often they escaped infection or had mild cases, thanks to immunities built up over many generations. Once the germs were released, however, the diseases raced ahead of them, carried by infected Indians. Every jungle trail, mountain road, and balsa became a highway for spreading infection. Indians, lacking any immunity, sickened and died without knowing why.

The disease struck Cuzco first, killing Huayna Capac's sister-wife and an estimated two hundred thousand others. Prayers were offered in all the temples and victims sacrificed, but to no avail. The infection spread to Quito, where it took the Sapa Inca himself. As he lay dying at Tumibamba, he called together his chiefs and wise men to hear his last words: "Our Father the Sun has revealed to me that after the reign of twelve Incas, his own children, there will appear in our country an unknown race of men who will subdue our Empire. I think that the people who came recently to our own shores are the ones referred to. They are strong, powerful men, who will outstrip you in everything. The reign of the twelve Incas ends with me. I can therefore certify to you that these people will return shortly after I have left you, and that they will accomplish what our father the Sun predicted they would."

The gods had spoken. The Land of the Four Quarters would perish in civil war and foreign conquest.

INCA AND SPANIARD

Pizarro and his men knew nothing of Huayna Capac's prophecy, but they were doing their best to make it come true. When their ship nosed into Panama harbor, townsmen rushed to greet those who'd been given up for dead. They were doubly excited when they saw their souvenirs and heard about the golden kingdom. But not Governor Rios. He was unimpressed "by the cheap display of gold and silver toys and a few Indian sheep." Too many lives had already been wasted, he said, and flatly refused to allow another voyage.

Once again Father Luque came to the rescue. If the king's representative wouldn't listen to them, then, said he, they must speak to his master. One of the partners would have to go to Spain to put their case before King Charles, grandson of Ferdinand and Isabella. Luque, the best educated, couldn't go because of religious duties. Almagro, short, one eyed, and illiterate, wouldn't have made a good impression at court. Pizarro, though uneducated, looked like a conquistador and could speak well when the spirit moved him. The others distrusted him, but felt he was the only man for the job. Pizarro, for his part, promised to look after their interests as if they were his own. "God grant, my children," said the priest, fixing his eyes on Pizarro, "that one of you may not defraud the others of his share!"

Pizarro crossed the Isthmus of Panama early in 1528 and boarded a ship at Nombre de Dios on the Caribbean coast. With him were Pedro de Candia, several Indians, two llamas, and a collection of gold ornaments and Peruvian fabrics. After an uneventful voyage, which pleased everyone, they anchored at Seville, Spain.

Pizarro was invited to visit the royal court in the city of Toledo. There he met Hernán Cortés, who'd recently returned to Spain on business. The cousins had much in common and spent hours discussing the conquest of Mexico. Pizarro, as we shall see, followed his cousin's example at least once, with stunning success.

King Charles gave Pizarro a warm welcome. A warrior himself, he was fascinated by tales of adventure in distant lands. More fascinating, however, were promises of gold, as his armies were costing him ever-increasing amounts. He approved Pizarro's plans and, after some delay, a Capitulation, or royal license, was issued July 26, 1529, for the conquest of Peru.

The Capitulation authorized Pizarro to recruit a 250-man army in Spain and the colonies. The army would seize New Castile, as Peru was known officially, and help convert the Indians to Christianity for the good of their souls; priests were to accompany the army always. As a reward for his efforts, Pizarro was made governor of New Castile and captain-general, commander of its armed forces, for life. He was also made a knight of the Order of Santiago with the right to a coat of arms. His shield bore the Pizarro family insignia, plus a Peruvian city with a ship and a llama. Almagro was made a hidalgo and named commander of the fortress of Tumbes; Luque became Bishop of Tumbes and "Protector of the Peruvian Indians." Bartholomew Ruiz received the title "Grand Pilot of the South Sea" and the survivors of the Isle of the Cock became hidalgos.

King Charles, though most generous with others' property, contributed little of his own to the venture. The costs of the conquest were to be met by the three partners, who'd have to borrow whatever they needed. The salaries that went with each office were to be paid out of loot, after deducting the royal share of one-fifth. All the king gave was his blessing, his license, and some military supplies. Had it not been for the generosity of Hernán Cortés, the expedition might never have gotten underway.

Having received his Capitulation, Pizarro left for Trujillo. He was proud of himself, and, although his parents had died years before, he wanted to show everyone that he'd "become someone." There was also the practical purpose of gathering fighting men. But most of Extremadura's bravest sons had already left for King Charles's wars and Pizarro found few volunteers; he only recruited about one hundred men in Spain.

INCA AND SPANIARD

Among the volunteers were his four half brothers, a nasty bunch even by the standards of the day. As one who'd known them said, "They were as proud as they were poor, and as much without wealth as eager to gain it." Like Francisco himself, Juan, twenty-two, and Gonzalo, twenty, were his father's sons, illegitimate and illiterate. Hernando, thirty, was old Gonzalo's only legitimate child. Tall and heavyset, with thick lips and a red nose, he was the only brother who'd received an education. Hernando was clever, brave, and ruthless, and was hated by everyone except his brothers. He went out of his way to make enemies; he liked to insult people in words touched with acid. When still a youngster, his father had taken him to the wars against the French, where he became a captain of infantry. He was the only officer on the expedition to have commanded in large-scale European battles, and Francisco trusted him completely. Pizarro's fourth half brother, Martin de Alcantara, twenty, was his mother's son by another man, also not her husband.

The brothers were joined by Pedro Pizarro, their fifteen-year-old cousin. Pedro was not only a soldier but a historian. Despite hardships, he kept detailed notes on everything he saw. His book, *Relation of the Discovery and Conquest of the Kingdom of Peru,* is the best firsthand account we have of these events.

The expedition left Spain in three small ships in January 1530. Arriving at Nombre de Dios, they found Almagro and Luque waiting. Soon after Pizarro stepped ashore, his two partners knew their doubts about him had been justified. Almagro lost his temper, accusing Pizarro of double-dealing. He'd taken every important office for himself, Almagro shouted, the veins bulging in his throat. As he spoke, the Pizarros stood by, smirking, their hands on their swords. Hernando even made some unkind, but true, remarks about Almagro's parentage. Had it not been for the priest, there would have been bloodshed then and there.

Luque now used all his powers of persuasion. After much discussion, Pizarro agreed not to give any offices to his brothers

Francisco Pizarro, Almagro, and some of the volunteers Pizarro recruited in Spain. Notice their armor and the flag of Castile. They are carrying halberds, spears with battle-axes attached.

until the partners were satisfied. All loot was to be shared equally among the partners. Finally, he promised to ask the king to grant Almagro a separate territory to rule once Peru was conquered.

The quarrel was patched up—for the time being. But from that day on, Almagro and the Pizarros hated one another. In time that hatred would lead to murder.

3

THE MEN
OF CAJAMARCA

PANAMA CITY, DECEMBER 27, 1530.

Excitement gripped this usually quiet seaport. Since dawn, sailors had been moving tons of supplies piled at dockside. Sweating and cursing, they'd tossed bundles and barrels and bales of every description aboard boats to be rowed out to the three ships rocking in the gentle swells. There was also live animal cargo—mostly pigs and chickens—to provide a continuing supply of fresh meat during the expedition. Thirty-seven horses were later hoisted aboard in large slings, for no army could be without them.

The cathedral was ablaze with candles in honor of the Christmas season and for the solemn religious service that was in progress. Francisco Pizarro and Diego de Almagro knelt with one hundred eighty others, praying for divine mercy. Father Luque solemnly blessed their venture with the sign of the cross. When he finished, they marched to the waterfront. Townspeople cheered, church bells clanged, trumpets blared, bidding them farewell and Godspeed. A soldier led the way with a banner showing Saint James as a knight in shining armor. They were going on a crusade against the heathen, and, God willing, they'd save souls and enrich themselves by doing His work.

Pizarro knew he was setting out to conquer a vast empire and that he'd have to fight armies larger than his own. Yet, though his army was small, it was a formidable fighting machine. His soldiers were as tough as any to be found anywhere in the Americas. Young men, mainly in their late twenties and early thirties, they were seasoned veterans of European wars and of countless Indian fights. The bulk of the soldiers came from Extremadura and Andalusia, its southern neighbor, and, like their leader, were illiterate or barely able to write their names. They served without pay, in return for a share of the booty. Pirates served under exactly the same terms.

What the soldiers lacked in numbers, they made up for in discipline and morale. Acting together, they obeyed a single will—Francisco Pizarro's. Unity, obedience, cooperation, teamwork: These balanced the odds, making the difference between victory and disaster.

Conquistadores also had the most advanced weapons of the age. Their bodies were protected by suits of armor made of steel plates hinged to allow freedom of movement. On their heads each wore a steel helmet with a long steel brim that rose to a graceful point at the front and back. A complete suit of armor weighed about sixty pounds, but since the weight was distributed evenly over the whole body, it was more comfortable than the sixty-pound backpack of today's American soldier. Spanish infantry might also wear shirts of chain mail, thousands of tiny steel rings joined together. Flexible and light, weighing from fourteen to thirty pounds, chain mail could turn away any stone- or copper-tipped spear.

Pizarro's men had an assortment of missile weapons for fighting at a distance. The harquebus was a gun with a three- to five-foot barrel. Unwieldy and difficult to load, it fired a lead ball, as did the falconet, the smallest type of cannon. The crossbow was a short bow mounted on a wooden stock and powered by twisted strings released by a trigger. As powerful as any gun, it could drive a steel-tipped arrow through a suit of armor. Although less accurate than the Indian's sling, these weapons were far deadlier. Anyone hit with a bullet or a crossbow arrow might be torn apart by the impact.

All battles, however, were decided at close quarters, and for this there was nothing like cold steel. Each man wore a dagger and a sword on his belt. Created by master craftsmen, the Spanish sword was a weapon without peer. It was made of Toledo steel, said to be the strongest and most flexible in the world. When finished, each new blade was bent into an S and struck hard against a steel helmet. If the blade passed the test, it was decorated with an etched design and a motto such as: "Never unsheathed in vain" or "For my lady and my King, this is my law." A yard long, light, flexible, and razor sharp, the Spanish sword was a fearsome weapon. A good swordsman—and Spaniards prided themselves on being the best—could lop off a head with one stroke.

The horse was to the conquistadores what the tank is to the modern army. Cavalry patrols covered great distances swiftly, carrying messages and helping the army avoid ambushes. The horse's speed and mobility made it possible to deliver attacks with devastating force. A horse and a rider in full armor weighed nearly a ton. Galloping at twenty miles an hour, the entire weight was concentrated at the tip of a diamond-shaped steel point at the end of a ten-foot lance. The cavalry was irresistible, except to other cavalry and specially trained infantry. Once cavalrymen got in among foot soldiers, the horsemen would use their greater height to strike downward with the sword. A solid blow from above could break through chain mail, splitting a man from collarbone to waist.

At Pizarro's signal, the three-ship fleet put to sea; as usual, Almagro stayed behind to gather reinforcements. After two weeks of bucking strong headwinds, the ships anchored in the bay of San Mateo just north of the equator. Although Tumbes lay three hundred fifty miles beyond, Pizarro put his army ashore and, with the ships keeping pace, began to march south. Why he did this is

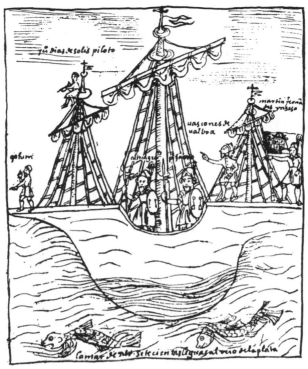

One of Pizarro's ships as seen by an Indian artist. The vessel must be close to shore, for the man seated atop the foremast is the pilot, whose job was to guide the ship through the shallows.

a mystery, since his route lay across unexplored swamps and jungle. Luckily, the exhausting march produced some profit when the Spaniards found an Indian village. Attacking without warning, they killed all who opposed them and drove the others into the jungle. A search turned up large quantities of gold and silver in the abandoned huts. Pizarro was overjoyed, but also practical. After dividing the loot among his men and setting aside the "royal fifth," he sent the ships back to Panama with a chest full of precious metals. This, he hoped, would speed up the reinforcements.

His soldiers, however, threw away much of their newfound wealth. In the loot were scores of emeralds, dark green beauties large as hens' eggs. Simple men, the soldiers listened to Father Reginaldo de Pedraza when he said that real emeralds were too hard to be broken. One after another, they crushed the emeralds with hammers, declaring them worthless. Not the priest. He later sold his own "worthless stones" at high prices in Panama, teaching everyone about the law of supply and demand.

For the sake of a quick profit, Pizarro lost the Indians' goodwill and the element of surprise. During the next four months, there were no more gold and emeralds, only suffering and death. The heat and humidity were all but unbearable. His men sweltered in their armor as puddles of sweat sloshed about in their boots. Men fainted, dropped to the ground, and lay where they fell. It was now the invaders' turn to suffer from a New World disease— verruca. A painful, wasting infection caused by a virus, verruca causes warts the size and color of purple figs that dangle from one's eyebrows, ears, nostrils, forehead, and cheeks.

After many hardships, the Spaniards arrived on the coast opposite the island of Puna fifty miles north of Tumbes. On the beach they met natives of Puna, who invited them to visit their island. Pizarro accepted the invitation and the army crossed on balsas.

They had been on Puna only a day when two balsas filled with warriors arrived from Tumbes. They'd come, an orejon explained, to pay their respects to the white chief. The Puna Indians stood by sullenly, glaring at the visitors, their age-old enemies. No one could remember a time when their peoples had been at peace, nor, indeed, did they wish for such a time. Hatred between them was a tradition, passed on from generation to generation, like a dance or ceremony.

Speaking through Felipillo, the orejon warned that the islanders couldn't be trusted. The moment the Spaniards lowered their guard, he said, they'd be killed and eaten, for the Punans were cannibals. That's all Pizarro had to hear. Without further ado, he handed over several Puna chieftains to their enemies, who beheaded them on the spot. The result was a bloody war in which stone-tipped spears proved no match for gunpowder and cavalry. Defeated in open combat, the Punans began a guerrilla war of ambushes and hit-and-run raids.

Good news came when Hernando de Soto arrived from Nicaragua with two ships carrying a hundred men and twenty-seven horses. De Soto, another extremeño, was said to be a fine gentleman and the best horseman in Spain. But he was also a cruel man who cared nothing for Indian lives. Years later, as the discoverer of the Mississippi River, he'd chop off the hands of any Indian who could not, or would not, lead him to gold.

At last Pizarro felt strong enough to go after a big prize. On May 16, 1532, his army landed near Tumbes. He'd always been friendly with the men of Tumbes and meant to use that friendship to take them by surprise. But they surprised him instead. The first three Spaniards ashore were met by smiling Indians, who promptly cut them to pieces. Their comrades, meantime, were attacked as they came ashore by hundreds of screaming warriors. At that moment Hernando Pizarro was nearing the beach in a balsa. Without hesitating, he sprang into the saddle and charged through the water. The Indians, who'd never seen a horse, fled, allowing the Spaniards to land their main force.

A worse surprise followed. Instead of a wealthy city waiting to be looted, the Spaniards found Tumbes a burned-out ruin. They moved through silent streets choked with rubble, hearing only their own footsteps. Houses with caved-in roofs and tumbled-down walls cast crazy shadows. Not an Indian was to be seen anywhere, nor was there a trace of the two men left behind during Pizarro's second voyage. And the temples—those gorgeous, gold-plated temples—had been stripped bare. For men who'd marched through hundreds of miles of jungle, driven by visions of a golden land, this was a terrible disappointment.

The reason for their misfortune became clear when a patrol captured the governor of Tumbes. He explained that his city had been wrecked and its people scattered during the War of the Two Brothers, a civil war that was still going on. With the central government weakened by the war, lawless men roamed the land, looting and killing as they pleased. It was they who'd attacked the Spaniards on the beach and killed the two men Pizarro had left behind.

Huayna Capac's prophecy was coming true.

As Huayna Capac had lay dying, he'd done something no Sapa Inca had ever done before. He had divided the empire. The largest part, plus the Sapa Inca's throne, went to Huáscar, "Good Fortune," his son by his chief sister-wife. The kingdom of Quito he willed to Atahuallpa, "Royal and Victorious Turkey Cock," his son by Tocto Coca. Atahuallpa was his favorite, and he loved him as he'd loved his mother. He'd pampered the boy by feeding him with his own sacred hands and took him on all his campaigns. The boy proved to be a natural soldier and quickly became a great general. No doubt, had it been possible, Huayna Capac would have given him the entire empire. But by leaving him Quito, with its warlike people and the veteran army stationed there, he'd given him the means of taking the whole empire if he chose. Yet Atahuallpa might never have tried to seize power had Huáscar not lost his self-control.

Huáscar was a spiteful person believed by some to be insane. He knew but one punishment for those who disappointed him: death. He is said to have ordered the massacre of all men and women in two towns near Cuzco for a minor offense. As Sapa Inca, he demanded again and again that Atahuallpa come to Cuzco for their father's funeral and to witness Huáscar's coronation. Atahuallpa, fearing for his life, refused to leave Quito. It was like squirting gasoline into a fire. Each refusal enraged Huáscar, until the mere mention on his half brother's name threw him into a tantrum.

Huáscar's anger exploded early in 1532. Atahuallpa had sent ambassadors to Cuzco with gifts worthy of a Sapa Inca. The ambassadors were to offer his regrets for not appearing in person and to reassure Huáscar of his loyalty. Huáscar, however, lost his temper and his dignity. While the court stood by with downcast eyes, he had the gifts burned and several of the ambassadors tortured to death. The others were stripped, dressed as women, and sent back to their master with women's clothes for him to wear. Huáscar's ancestors had fought many wars, but never had they murdered ambassadors. Such behavior was unthinkable; indeed, uncivilized.

Huáscar followed up this insult by sending an army led by General Huanca Auqui, "Field-Guardian Prince." That was a mistake. Huanca Auqui was a good soldier, but no match for Atahuallpa. At the first news of Huanca Auqui's coming, Atahuallpa mobilized his veterans under two of his father's ablest commanders. The first, Chalcuchima, had never lost a major battle. His comrade, Quizquiz, "Little Bird," was nothing like his name. Ferocious in battle, Quizquiz showed no mercy to the defeated.

Atahuallpa's generals showed their skill outside Tumibamba. They slaughtered Huanca Auqui's army in a two-day battle and hurled the remnants southward in panicky retreat. Between fifteen and sixteen thousand warriors were killed and their bodies left to rot; years later, Spaniards wrote about mounds of bleached bones littering the battlefield. Several captured officers were tortured, beheaded, and their skulls made into drinking cups for Atahuallpa's enjoyment.

Atahuallpa had been so insulted that his vengeance knew no bounds. All who'd opposed him, all who'd favored his brother, were doomed. Tumibamba was the main city of the Cañari tribe, who'd served the Sapa Incas for generations. Since the Cañari sided with Huáscar, Atahuallpa vowed to wipe them from the face of the earth. When Tumibamba fell, the survivors were herded into a nearby field. Men, women, and children were butchered before Atahuallpa's eyes. Their city was leveled, so that scarcely one stone remained on top of another. For good measure, he had every Cañari village in the area destroyed, along with its inhabitants.

Atahuallpa followed up his victory with a full-scale invasion of Peru. Once he set his armies in motion, they were irresistible. Huáscar's forces crumbled before them, spreading panic as they streamed southward.

Chasquis raced from Cuzco in every direction with the Sapa Inca's orders. War drums called men to arms throughout the Land of the Four Quarters. Within a few weeks, Huáscar had gathered the largest army in Inca history to defend Cuzco. There were warriors from the Lake Titicaca area, Bolivia, Chile, Argentina, and the jungles of the Eastern Cordillera. Each people wore its own costume, turning the Valley of Cuzco into a sea of brilliant banners and feather capes. Drums throbbed, echoing off the mountainsides; flutes of human bone made shrill music; men sang of victory.

Yet, large as it was, Huáscar's army was made up mostly of raw recruits. Worse, Atahuallpa's veterans had the habit of success. They'd won every battle thus far, which made their confidence soar as they neared Cuzco.

The enemy awaited them at the Cotapampa River, the last natural barrier before the capital. Huáscar now called upon the gods to help one Inca army destroy another. On a hill overlooking the river, he summoned a grand convention of huacas. Every sacred stone, piece of wood, and idol that could be found within a hundred miles was carried to the hilltop and set in a circle. With the army watching from below, he joined the priests in begging the gods' favor. Scores of handsome boys were then brought before the huacas. They staggered along, drunk on chicha and coca, guided by priests. As each walked around an idol for the third time, a priest slipped a cord around his neck and pulled hard. The little body was then tumbled into a shallow grave nearby, along with golden ornaments for its spirit to take to the next world.

The two armies met on a plain covered with tall grass. Huáscar, feeling the wind at his back, ordered the grass set on fire. Flames crackled in hundreds of places at once, and suddenly Atahuallpa's veterans were caught in an inferno. They screamed as wind-whipped flames set their hair and clothes afire. They broke ranks, pursued by Huáscar's men, who stabbed them from behind and killed the wounded as they lay on the ground. Huáscar could have won then and there. But instead of annihilating the enemy while he had the chance, he called back his troops. The invaders were beaten, he thought. There'd be time enough to finish them tomorrow. Tonight was for celebrating and for thanking the gods.

Chalcuchima and Quizquiz had no intention of waiting to be slaughtered. Under cover of darkness they rallied their troops and hid them along the sides of a ravine near the battlefield. At sunup one of Huáscar's generals led his men into the trap. They were killed and their general captured. Quizquiz tortured the general into revealing that his master would soon come down that same ravine with a larger force. Huáscar did. The men of Cuzco were taken by surprise and easily defeated. Huáscar was riding in his litter when the trap closed. Chalcuchima himself leaped forward and, cutting his way through the bodyguard, dragged the Son of the Sun to the ground.

Chalcuchima now reached deeply into his bag of tricks. He climbed into the litter and had himself carried toward the enemy's base camp. There were tens of thousands of warriors in that camp, waiting for orders. When they saw the imperial litter approach, followed by an army, they thought the victory had already been won. A victory *had* been won, but it wasn't theirs. Drawing closer, Chalcuchima struck with such speed and ferocity that the enemy fled in panic. Some kept running until they reached Cuzco. The sight of them, bleeding, dirty, and with torn clothes, horrified the people. Never had the Land of the Four Quarters suffered such a disaster; it was said that 150,000 Indians died at the Cotapampa.

"Anay ananay!" people cried, "Woe! Woe!" Little did they know that the worst was yet to come.

Atahuallpa had decided to make himself the Sapa Inca. But since he had no right to the throne, he had to eliminate all possible sources of opposition. Anyone who had, or might later have, a claim to the throne had to die. In addition, anyone who'd served Huáscar, or knew the history of his reign, or anyone who could threaten him in any way was marked for death.

Chalcuchima and Quizquiz were experts at mass killing. The moment Atahuallpa's forces occupied Cuzco, they began a reign of terror. Those who'd made the quipus for Huáscar's reign were killed, as were all their servants and families, so as to erase the past. Huáscar's uncles, cousins, and nephews were hunted like wild beasts. All were treated as common criminals, clubbed to death, hung by the heels, or crushed under rocks. Two hundred of Huáscar's brothers, the sons of Huayna Capac, met the same fate.

Chalcuchima's and Quizquiz's last action was even more horrible. Huáscar was tied to a frame of poles and brought to where his women had been assembled. Then, before his eyes, his wives, concubines, and children were killed one by one. "Ah!" he cried to the Inca gods. "You who raised me up for so short a time, now bring it to pass that he who forces me to witness such things, should be himself so treated!" When the slaughter was over, the mangled bodies were impaled on wooden posts as an example to others. Huáscar himself, his queen, and his mother were saved for torture to be supervised by Atahuallpa in person.

Atahuallpa, meantime, was at Cajamarca, "Canyon City," six hundred miles to the north. With the war over, he was enjoying the hot-spring baths and planning his coronation. As he was about to leave for Cuzco, a chasqui brought a message from the coast. The Bearded Ones had returned and were in Tumbes.

The War of the Two Brothers was welcome news to Francisco Pizarro. Had he tried to invade Peru earlier, he would have

Huáscar led away as a captive by Generals Quizquiz and Chalcuchima. The people of Cuzco were amazed at this sight, for never before had a Sapa Inca been treated with such disrespect.

been met by a united empire. Things were different now. Although the civil war had just ended, the land was still in turmoil. Many people considered Huáscar the true Son of the Sun and despised Atahuallpa as a criminal. The Inca were split, giving Pizarro the opportunity to play off one side against the other.

Early in June 1532, Pizarro left Tumbes and marched eighty miles to the south. Arriving in the Chiara Valley, he founded a settlement called San Miguel de Tangarara. The settlement, complete with a church, a fort, and a town hall, was to serve a twofold purpose. It would keep open his line of communication with Panama and be the springboard for his advance into the interior.

During the next three months, Pizarro turned San Miguel de

Tangarara into a secure rear-base area. Cavalry units were sent on long patrols to explore the country and win the Indians' loyalty. Each patrol was accompanied by a priest, who taught about Christianity. No looting was allowed, or violence, unless absolutely necessary. But when necessary, the violence was calculated to inspire fear. Any chief who resisted the Spaniards was burned alive before his people.

Hernando de Soto led a patrol into the upper Chiara Valley, to the foothills of the Western Cordillera. There he saw ruined villages and Indians hung by the feet, victims of the recent fighting. He also learned that the new Sapa Inca was camped with an army at Cajamarca. That city lay in a valley nine thousand feet above sea level, a journey of only three hundred and fifty miles from San Miguel de Tangarara.

For Pizarro, that journey was to be a leap into the unknown. All he knew was that he would enter a vast, mysterious land to meet the dreaded Atahuallpa. He may not have even had a definite plan, hoping to take advantage of situations as they arose. But one thing is certain: He'd come too far to turn back. He was in his sixty-first year. He'd given eight years of his life, eight years of toil and worry, to reach this point. This was his last chance.

On September 24, 1532, Pizarro assembled his army outside the settlement. The tiny force numbered 110 infantry, 67 cavalry, plus several hundred Indian porters; 50 soldiers would be left behind to hold the settlement. With his brother Hernando at his side, Pizarro rode along the ranks, reviewing the troops. He must have been deeply moved, for he said nothing. He simply stood in his stirrups and, drawing his sword, pointed to the towering Andes. So began the conquest of Peru.

The army moved in a southeasterly direction. At first, the going was easy. Wherever it passed, friendly Indians offered food and shelter. After a week, the army paused for a few days while Pizarro separated the men from the boys. He knew that some would lose courage when things got rough and that cowards are troublemakers, who undermine discipline. To avoid problems later, he offered to allow anyone who wished to return to San Miguel de Tangarara to do so without loss of honor. Nine men took the offer, leaving the legendary one hundred sixty-eight "Men of Cajamarca."

Continuing their march, they began to climb the foothills of the Western Cordillera, a beautiful country of fertile valleys and agricultural terraces. In one of these valleys, at the village of Zarán, they were met by an orejon whose clothes and manners marked him as an official of the highest rank. He explained that the lord Atahuallpa had sent him to greet the strangers and invite them to visit him at Cajamarca. Promising that everything would be done to make their journey comfortable, he gave Pizarro gifts of cloth embroidered with golden threads and a perfume made of dried goose flesh. In return, Pizarro gave him a Holland shirt, a red cap, and two glass cups for his master, adding that he came in peace.

The communications system built by the Inca to extend their empire served its invaders equally well. The Spaniards marched along the royal roads, shaded by overhanging trees and refreshed by streams flowing alongside. At night they camped at the royal storehouses, where they were received as honored guests.

The Indians were fascinated by the bearded white men, thinking them visitors from the sky. But what interested them even more were the horses. They didn't know what to make of these mighty creatures; they were at least the equals of their riders, who spoke sweetly to them, fed them, and combed their hair every evening.

One day, Indians watched some horses champing at their bits. Noting that the bits were made of iron, they decided it was the horses' food. Bowing deeply, the Indians backed away, returning moments later with bars of gold and silver. These they placed on the ground before the horses and, bowing again, said: "Do leave your iron aside, and eat this fodder, which is much better!" When the Indians turned their backs, the Spaniards took away the "fodder." The horses liked their food, they told the Indians, but wanted more, otherwise they'd become angry and gobble them up.

The advance grew more difficult with each passing day. Pleasant valleys gave way to barren, windswept mountainsides. Higher, higher they climbed, until they could see clouds *beneath* them. All around them were ranks of snowcapped mountains jutting through clouds. At these elevations the air was so thin and so clear that the sunlight hurt their eyes. The cold made them shiver in their armor. Soldiers gasped for breath and felt their chests tighten. Gradually, though, they became used to the heights and breathed easier.

The road, however, became more difficult. It was so steep in places that Inca engineers had cut gigantic staircases into the mountainsides. Narrowing, it twisted and turned along rock ledges. Loose rocks fell over the edge, but no echo came from below. When the Spaniards had to cross a rope bridge, the most stouthearted adventurers trembled. Many, giddy at the height, crawled across the swaying bridge on all fours with closed eyes.

Roads often passed beneath stone watchtowers, and every mountain pass was guarded by a fort. How high they seemed! And frightening! A few Indians could easily have rolled down boulders, burying the Spaniards beneath tons of debris or sending them hurtling into a gorge. In passing these man-made obstacles, the Spaniards felt naked and defenseless. Hernando Pizarro recalled one pass: "The road was so bad that they could very easily have taken us there or at another pass which we found between here and Cajamarca. For we could not use the horses on the roads, not even with skill, and off the roads we could take neither horses nor foot-soldiers." Unable to attack or defend, they were at the Indians' mercy.

Yet these outposts were always unmanned and the Spaniards passed unopposed. As they passed, a question must have flashed into each soldier's mind: Why was Atahuallpa allowing them into the heart of his domain?

It was a good question, and we shall never be certain of the answer. There are several possible explanations. It may not have occurred to Atahuallpa that he need fear these strangers, let alone that they'd try to conquer the Inca. After all, he was a god surrounded by a victorious army. At the slightest sign of trouble, the armies of Chalcuchima and Quizquiz could come racing back from Cuzco.

Superstitious peasants might think the strangers were sky-beings, but the Son of the Sun knew better. Gods wouldn't have allowed themselves to be killed, as these had been during the landing at Tumbes. Gods had limitless power, but the strangers' weapons were toys. Atahuallpa believed this because spies, who'd never seen the Spaniards in action, sent back confused reports. They assured him that unsaddled horses were harmless, and could not fight at night. Guns took a long time to reload and could fire only two shots, they said. Spanish swords were no deadlier than the sticks women used in weaving. These reports made Atahuallpa burn with curiosity to see the strangers. And, like the cat, his curiosity killed him.

On the morning of Friday, November 15, 1532, Francisco Pizarro rounded a bend in the road and reined in his horse. Spread before him, two thousand feet below, was the Valley of Cajamarca. His objective, the town of Cajamarca, glistened as the sun played on thatched roofs. A river meandered through the lush fields beyond. Clouds of vapor from hot springs drifted across the valley or clung to the surrounding mountainsides.

What Pizarro saw on one mountainside took his breath away. The slopes were white with the tents of an army of at least fifty thousand men. The memory of that camp was vivid years later for the soldier Juan Ruiz de Arce: "The Indians' camp looked like a very beautiful city. So many were the tents that we were filled with fright. We never thought the Indians could occupy such a proud position, nor so many tents, so well set up. It filled all us Spaniards with confusion and fear. But we dared not show it, much less turn back, for if they sensed the least weakness in us, the very Indians we brought with us would have killed us. So with a show of good spirits . . . we descended into the valley below and entered the town of Cajamarca."

Cajamarca was a large, well built town with a population of ten thousand. In addition to the Sapa Inca's palace and a Temple of the Sun, it had two stone forts. The larger fort stood on a rise and was surrounded by a triple ring of walls; the smaller fort occupied a corner of a plaza. The plaza was enclosed on three sides by walls of adobe, sunbaked clay bricks. Its fourth side consisted of three stone buildings with doors opening onto the plaza. These had housed the garrison, but were now empty, as was the town itself. The only sounds the conquistadores heard as they marched through the streets were the patter of their horses' hooves and the jangle of their own armor. The quiet gave them a sense of foreboding, as if something terrible was about to happen.

As soon as guards were posted, Pizarro sent his brother Hernando and Hernando de Soto to the Indian camp with a cavalry escort. They were to invite Atahuallpa to dinner and, if possible, discover his intentions.

They set out across the valley at a fast trot. All wore armor and sat tall in the saddle. They didn't dare show fear, but came on with trumpets blaring and weapons clashing. Splashing across a shallow stream, they rode along avenues of tents, past columns of spearmen and warriors with spiked maces. The warriors frowned, but let them pass.

Atahuallpa met them outside a large pavilion of red cloth laced with golden threads. A man of about thirty, he was tall, stout, and strongly built. Bloodshot eyes made him look ferocious. He was seated on a low stool, surrounded by orejones arranged according to their rank. Women squatted on the ground at his feet, and a bodyguard of four hundred warriors stood behind him. Although his face showed no expression, he radiated authority. The Spaniards knew instinctively that this man knew how to command and expected obedience.

96

Hernando Pizarro and Hernando de Soto meet Atahuallpa. In reality, when they met, Atahuallpa was seated outside his tent, not being borne in a litter.

Hernando Pizarro rode up to Atahuallpa and doffed his helmet. Without dismounting, he had Felipillo say that he'd come in friendship and to invite Atahuallpa to dinner with his brother, the Spanish commander. Atahuallpa, who'd been sitting silently with his head bowed and eyes fixed on the ground, looked up. A faint smile crossed his lips as he said that he was fasting, but would visit tomorrow; meantime, let the Spaniards occupy the buildings on the plaza. Atahuallpa's statement was as much a lie as Francisco Pizarro's offer of friendship. November 15 was no fast day for the Inca.

97

INCA AND SPANIARD

As Atahuallpa spoke, he kept glancing sideways at de Soto's horse, a spirited charger that kept champing at the bit. Seeing his interest in the animal, de Soto gave an exhibition of horsemanship that amazed even his comrades. Clapping spurs to the horse's sides, he galloped down the avenue of tents. The horse pranced, reared, and jumped. Then, turning toward the royal pavilion, de Soto raced forward at top speed. Bystanders dove for cover as horse and rider tore past, showering them with clods of earth.

Not the Sapa Inca. He sat on his stool, impassive, never moving a muscle. De Soto kept coming, faster, faster, until the last moment, when he reined in the horse, forcing it back on its haunches. The animal was so close to Atahuallpa that its breath rustled his hair and foam from its mouth stained his clothes. But Atahuallpa expected his men to be as brave as himself. After the Spaniards left, those Inca who had fled from de Soto's horse, among them several high officials who were relatives, were beheaded, together with their wives and children.

After De Soto's display, women now appeared with golden vessels full of chicha. The horsemen drank heartily and took their leave. Hernando Pizarro recalled that the ride back was anything but cheerful. They rode silently, gloomily, for they'd seen the face of death. These Inca were not the mobs of undisciplined savages they were used to fighting, but a disciplined war machine. As the sun set behind the mountains, an icy wind lashed the riders with rain and sleet, further dampening their spirits.

Back at Cajamarca, Pizarro called his officers to discuss their next move. There were few choices. They could stay put, trusting to Atahuallpa's good nature, a foolish move given what they knew about the War of the Two Brothers. Retreat would show fear, inviting attack; besides, the forts they'd passed had surely been reoccupied. Open battle would be suicidal.

After his officers had discussed and rejected each option, Pizarro presented his own plan. That plan may well have taken shape in his mind during his conversations with Hernán Cortés four years earlier. Cortés, too, had found himself outnumbered and with retreat cut off. He'd solved the problem by a stunning act of treachery against the Indians' leader. One day he'd led a squad of soldiers into the palace of Montezuma, the Aztec emperor. Montezuma had been given an offer he couldn't refuse: either he became the Spaniards' "guest," or they knifed him on the spot. He had accepted, and by so doing became Cortés' insurance policy. Montezuma had continued to rule the Aztecs, while Cortés ruled Montezuma. Pizarro meant to do the same with Atahuallpa. Only this time there'd be bloodshed, for the Sapa Inca would be surrounded by thousands of men eager to lay down their lives for him.

By now Cajamarca lay in darkness. Across the valley, the Inca camp blazed with lights. "It looked like a sky thick with stars," a Spaniard recalled.

Few in Cajamarca slept that night. Soldiers spent the long hours on their knees in prayer, or confessing their sins to the priests. They sharpened swords, checked crossbows, and primed their harquebuses. Everyone, officers and men alike, took a turn at guard duty. Pizarro visited the outposts over and over again. He knew everyone by name, and the sound of his voice reassured them. But his message was always the same: "Make fortresses of your hearts for you have no other." Tomorrow they'd have only their Spanish courage and Toledo steel. If these failed, they were goners.

Dawn, Saturday, November 16, 1532, found the conquistadores at their posts. The cavalry, led by both Hernandos—Pizarro and de Soto—waited in two of the barracks, which had high, wide doorways that would allow them to charge out instantly. The infantry was stationed in the third barracks, while harquebusiers and crossbowmen hid between the buildings. They were to remain under cover until Pizarro waved a white scarf. At that signal, Pedro de Candia, who covered the plaza from the upper fortress with two falconets, would open fire and the troops would come out fighting. While they massacred the Indians, Pizarro and twenty picked men would seize the Sapa Inca.

Atahuallpa, however, was in no hurry to keep his appointment. He was the Sapa Inca, and lowly creatures like Spaniards must wait on his pleasure. But for those in the barracks, waiting increased the tension that is always felt before battle.

Not until late in the afternoon did a lookout give the alarm. The Inca were coming not by the hundreds, but by the thousands. Their advance guard, ten thousand strong, carried maces and slings. Behind them came ranks of spearmen in battle array. When Pizarro sent an interpreter to learn why they were armed, Atahuallpa said that, since the Spaniards had brought weapons into his camp, he'd do the same. That worried Pizarro, who'd planned an ambush, not a battle. Nevertheless, he sent word that Atahuallpa would be welcome "as a friend and a brother" no matter how he came.

The procession moved slowly, filling the road and the meadows on either side for hundreds of yards in all directions. In the center of this mass of humanity was the royal household, with Atahuallpa borne on a litter.

Occasionally, lookouts whispered to their hidden comrades. The procession was coming closer, they reported. It had crossed the river and was heading straight for them along the road.

The tension inside the barracks became unbearable. Soldiers gripped weapons tightly, their knuckles turning white. Pedro Pizarro's records tell us his comrades were so frightened that they wet their pants: "I saw many of the Spaniards urinate without noticing it out of sheer terror."

A half-mile from Cajamarca, the procession suddenly halted and began to pitch tents. Soon an Indian brought word that his master had changed his plans; he'd camp for the night and visit Pizarro in the morning.

We cannot be certain why Atahuallpa decided to stop. Perhaps he suspected a trap; not a Spaniard had been seen during the day, although they were known to be in the town. Perhaps he was deliberately stalling; for with night approaching, the Spaniards' horses would be powerless.

Whatever the reason, Pizarro was frantic. His men, he knew, were exhausted from their journey and a sleepless night. Another such night would be too much even for them. In desperation, he sent word that all was ready and that he would be disappointed if Atahuallpa didn't come as promised. This was bitterly true, although what followed was a clever lie. He assured Atahuallpa that he could come without fear—not that such a brave warrior could be afraid. Even if Atahuallpa was suspicious, this challenge to his pride couldn't be ignored; he had to go.

Pizarro's messenger returned with better news than anyone expected. Not only would Atahuallpa keep his appointment, his warriors would stay outside Cajamarca. He'd come with only six thousand men, mostly orejones of the highest rank.

Inti, his Sun-god protector, was sinking behind the western mountains when the procession resumed. It was a breathtaking spectacle, the last the Inca would ever stage as an independent people. Although the meadows around Cajamarca swarmed with warriors, the royal party came unarmed. Leading the way were hundreds of servants in red and white robes, who examined every inch of roadway, removing loose pebbles and sweeping it clean with branches. If the road wasn't perfectly smooth, one of the Sapa Inca's litter bearers might fall, bringing bad luck. The Sapa Inca was so sacred that he must never touch the ground trod by common humanity.

Next came groups of dancers accompanied by musicians playing flutes, cymbals, drums, and conch-shell trumpets. Choruses chanted Atahuallpa's praises: "Oh, great and very powerful Lord, Son of the Sun, only ruler, may all the earth obey you." As the procession drew nearer, the chanting grew louder, sending a thrill of terror through the jittery Spaniards. One of them recalled that it "sounded like the songs of hell."

101

INCA AND SPANIARD

The procession streamed into the plaza through a single narrow gateway. Without a signal being given, the Indians moved to the right and left, forming a living corridor to the center of the plaza. The crowd fell silent as orejones with gold earplugs, gold bracelets, and gold plates on their chests came forward. Atahuallpa followed on a litter richer than any throne of Europe. It was covered with gold and silver plates studded with precious stones. Eighty of the highest orejones in the land carried it slowly, so as not to jar its passenger. Others walked alongside, shielding him with parasols of red, blue, and green feathers.

Like a true Son of the Sun, Atahuallpa glittered from head to toe. His short hair was covered with golden ornaments and he wore a collar of emeralds around his neck. His robe was of fine cloth embroidered with golden threads. On his right arm he carried a golden shield with an image of the sun. In his left hand he held a scepter of gold and silver, symbolic of the sun and moon. His sandals were of solid gold. Spaniards who managed to peep out of their hiding places could hardly believe their eyes.

When the litter reached the center of the plaza, Atahuallpa ordered a halt. Looking around, he saw everywhere the faces of his adoring subjects. But the Spaniards were nowhere in sight.

"Where are they?" he called out. "Where are the strangers?"

Suddenly, as if by magic, the strangest person he'd ever seen stepped from a doorway. This was Friar Vincente de Valverde, and he belonged to the Order of Saint Dominic, which preached to the common people in Europe. He wore no armor like a soldier, but a black hood, a white robe tied at the waist with a cord, and leather sandals. As he walked toward the glittering assembly, he held before him a wooden crucifix. He had a vital role to play in the tragedy about to unfold. According to Spanish law, Pizarro couldn't attack the Indians without fair warning. Before using armed force, he had to ask them to surrender and become Christians peacefully. Only if they refused, could he attack. The friar was about to make that request.

102

La conquista del Peru.

llamada la nueua Castilla. La ol tierra por diuina vo
luntad fue marauillosamente conquistada en la felicis
sima ventura del Emperador y Rey nuestro señor y
por la prudencia y esfuerço del muy magnifico y vale
roso cauallero el Capitan Francisco piçarro Gouerna
dor y adelantado de la nueua castilla y de su herma
no Hernando piçarro y de sus animosos capitanes
z fieles y esforçados compañeros. q̃ cõ el se hallaron'

Friar Valverde offers his Bible to Atahuallpa in the square of Cajamarca. The illustration is from the cover of *La Conquesta del Peru* (*The Conqest of Peru*), the first book on the subject, printed in 1534. A copy of this rare book is in the collection of the New York Public Library.

103

INCA AND SPANIARD

Speaking through an interpreter, Valverde recited the history of the world from the Creation to the present. He told of the One True God, the Holy Trinity, and the Crucifixion and Resurrection of Jesus Christ. He then explained how the Pope, God's deputy on earth, had ordered King Charles of Spain to conquer the peoples of the New World and convert them to Christianity. He ended by calling upon Atahuallpa to abandon idol worship and surrender to the king's representative, Francisco Pizarro. If he gave in willingly, the Land of the Four Quarters would become part of the Spanish Empire, the mightiest and holiest on earth. "But if you refuse," Valverde added, "you must know that we will make merciless war upon you, that all your idols will be cast down, and that fire and sword and bloodshed will compel you, whether you wish it or not, to reject your false religion, to receive our Catholic faith, pay tribute to our Emperor, and surrender your kingdom to him."

"Your emperor may be a great prince," said Atahuallpa, shaking with rage. "I do not doubt it . . . and I am willing to hold him as my brother. As for the Pope of whom you speak, he must be mad to talk of giving away countries that do not belong to him." Then, pointing to the sun, he proclaimed his faith in the religion of his fathers. "Your own god, as you tell me, was put to death by the very men he created. My god still lives in the heavens."

It was Valverde's turn to be shocked. Never in his life had he heard anyone talk like this—and live. He wouldn't have been surprised had fire and brimstone poured from heaven to consume this wicked pagan. Back home, where the Dominicans supervised the Spanish Inquisition, hundreds were burned alive each year for differing with the Church. The burning ceremony was called an *auto-da-fé*, an "act of faith."

Atahuallpa now asked by what right he made these outrageous demands. Valverde answered by holding up a Bible, which the Inca took into his hands.

He looked at it curiously, flipping the thin white leaves covered with black markings. If this Bible-huaca had any power, it should have spoken to him. But since all he heard was the swishing of paper, he threw it away, shouting, "This says nothing to me." The interpreter picked it up and returned it to Valverde, who ran toward the barracks.

"Come out! Come out, Christians!" he cried as he ran. "Come at these unfriendly dogs who reject the things of God. That chief has thrown on the ground the book of our sacred law." This was the moment the Spaniards had been waiting for. The Inca had rejected the Bible and now the Spaniards could attack with a clear conscience. Any bloodshed would be the fault of the Indians and not their own.

Pizarro stepped from a doorway and waved his white scarf. Instantly, falconets boomed and barrack doors flew open. As cannon balls whistled across the plaza, infantrymen spilled out of the barracks. The cavalry charged at top speed. The blare of trumpets mingled with bells and rattles attached to the horses' harness. Hooves pounded on the flagstones, striking sparks. Again and again, the Spanish war cry rose above the din: "Santiago! Santiago! Saint James and at them."

No Spaniard then or since has dared call what followed a battle. It was a massacre pure and simple. The Indians had only cloth tunics and feather capes against the Spaniards' weapons. Cannon balls scythed through the crowd, leaving a trail of mangled bodies in their wake. Harquebus bullets and crossbow arrows struck home, sometimes killing two men at a time. Indians, unable to get out of the horses' way, were tossed about like rag dolls or crushed under iron-shod hooves. Those trying to flee were ridden down from behind and lifted off the ground with a lance point jutting through the chest.

The plaza became a slaughter pen made slippery by rivulets of blood. Early in the attack, hundreds had been killed near its narrow gateway. Their comrades were so terrified that they rushed the gateway, trying to climb over the bodies. But instead of escap-

Théodore de Bry's interpretation of the massacre at Cajamarca. Spaniards wielding halberds and swords and firing harquebuses butchered at least two thousand unarmed Indians in order to seize the Sapa Inca, Atahuallpa.

ing, they formed huge mounds and suffocated each other. The wall of flesh blocked the escape route and prevented the warriors outside from coming to the rescue. In their panic, thousands pressed against the adobe wall until a fifteen-yard section collapsed under the weight of their bodies. The survivors then fled across the valley, spreading their panic and starting a stampede among the warriors. But the Spanish cavalry jumped the broken wall and galloped onto the plain. Driven wild with bloodlust, they kept after the Indians, shouting, "Do not let any escape!" and, "Spear them!" Hundreds were cut down as they ran.

106

Meantime, Pizarro and his men were carving a path through Atahuallpa's bodyguard. There was no panic here, only stubborn determination to protect their master at any cost. Unarmed men deliberately stepped between Atahuallpa and sword blades dripping with blood. They came forward by the hundreds, clinging to the Spaniards' sword arms until struck down themselves. Although the royal litter tossed and swayed, the orejones kept it aloft. Many had their hands cut off, but supported it with their shoulders during the moments of life remaining to them.

It was useless. The Spaniards cut their way forward and, grabbing the edge of the litter, turned it over, tossing Atahuallpa to the ground. As he fell, a soldier lunged at him with his sword. He would have been run through had Pizarro not taken the blow on his own hand. "Let no one wound the Indian upon pain of death," he shouted as he took him prisoner. In protecting the Sapa Inca, Pizarro became the only Spanish casualty.

The massacre of Cajamarca had taken less than an hour. During that time, the Spaniards killed between three and four thousand defenseless Indians. God, they believed, had allowed them to triumph against all odds. They were His warriors, crusaders in a holy war to rid the New World of paganism. Pedro Pizarro recorded that moment for posterity: "Then, night having come, all the Spaniards gathered together and gave thanks to our Lord for the mercies he had granted to them, and they were well content with having made prisoner the Lord [Atahuallpa], because, had they not taken him so, the land would not have been won as it was won."

The Spaniards lost no time in gathering the fruits of victory. Pizarro had Atahuallpa send word that the strangers would ride out of Cajamarca in the morning. Any Indian who did not carry a cross as a token of surrender would be killed where he stood.

Next morning, while the dead were being stripped of their valuables and buried, Hernando de Soto led thirty horsemen to the camp at the hot springs. As thousands of warriors looked on,

107

each holding a tiny wooden cross, the Spaniards ransacked the camp. They brought back golden drinking vessels and statues, golden bracelets, necklaces, and earplugs. In addition, they brought droves of llamas to be slaughtered for food.

Yet Atahuallpa's army still outnumbered his captors by hundreds to one. They could have attacked the Spaniards and tried to set the Sapa Inca free. At the very least they could have surrounded Cajamarca and let hunger do their work for them. Instead, they allowed themselves to be dispersed without a struggle. No warrior people ever gave up so easily.

Not that they were cowards. Far from it, as we've seen. Properly led, they and their ancestors had built an empire. Properly led! That was the key to their failure and to Pizarro's success. In a sense, the Land of the Four Quarters consisted of millions of hands directed by a single brain. The Inca had no idea of himself as a *citizen*, with rights as well as duties. Instead, he was a *subject*, existing only to obey and to serve the Sapa Inca. Always discouraged from thinking for himself, he was incapable of resistance at this moment of supreme crisis. Without the ruler's guidance, the people were confused, paralyzed, unable to show initiative. After Cajamarca, they didn't resist, because no one commanded them to do so. By seizing its head, Pizarro had seized the entire Inca Empire.

Pizarro treated his prisoner with respect, even kindness. He allowed Atahuallpa's women and servants to move into his quarters in the palace of Cajamarca. Inside these quarters, the Sapa Inca's word was law. He was still waited on hand and foot, still drank chicha from the skulls of his enemies. Orejones still came to him barefoot, carrying token burdens on their shoulders. He still gave them orders, which were immediately obeyed. The only difference was that important matters had to be cleared with Pizarro, whose guards stood outside Atahuallpa's door.

Atahuallpa, meanwhile, studied the ways of his captors.

Spanish officers taught him to play dice and chess, and soon he beat them at their own games. He was so intelligent that he could speak their language in twenty days. He even learned to read a little, which was more than the illiterate Pizarro could do. Atahuallpa did this by asking a man to write down certain words, then asking another man to read them back to him in private.

Atahuallpa quickly realized that the Spaniards craved gold above everything else. This puzzled him, as we'd be puzzled if invaders from Mars craved butterfly wings, beautiful though not valuable in themselves. Still he hoped to turn the Spaniards' greed to his own advantage.

One day he told Pizarro that he would give gold in return for his freedom.

"How much gold?" Pizarro asked.

Atahuallpa replied that he'd cover the floor of the room they were standing in with the yellow metal. Pizarro frowned. Surely the Indian was joking, and he saw nothing funny where gold was concerned.

Question and answer. The Indian asks: "Is it this gold which you eat?" The Spaniard replies: "Yes. We eat this gold." The Indians, who valued gold only for its beauty, couldn't understand the Spaniards' lust for the yellow metal.

109

Atahuallpa, misinterpreting Pizarro's reaction, raised the bid. If it was gold Pizarro wanted, he'd offer a ransom worthy of a living god. He'd fill the room with gold as high as he could reach. So saying, he stood on his toes while Pizarro painted a red line around the wall. Both the room and the line may still be seen in Cajamarca's Casa del Inca, "House of the Inca."

A contract was drawn up and signed by witnesses. In it Atahuallpa promised to fill a room twenty-two feet long by seventeen feet wide with gold to a height of nine feet. The gold was not to be in solid bars, but in the form it had been cast by the goldsmiths. For good measure, an adjoining room was to be filled twice over with articles of silver. The ransom was to be paid within two months, at the end of which time he would be freed.

Atahuallpa's contract with Pizarro became his half brother's death warrant. He feared that Huáscar, still held prisoner by Atahuallpa's generals, might offer the Spaniards a larger ransom for his own freedom. If Huáscar was freed, or if Pizarro decided that he was the rightful Sapa Inca, he, Atahuallpa, was doomed. To prevent this, he sent secret orders for killing the prisoners. Huáscar, his sister-wife, and their mother died under torture. Their bodies were then cut to bits and, according to legend, eaten by the executioners. Most likely the pieces were tossed into a swift river and carried to the Pacific.

Meanwhile, treasure began to arrive at Cajamarca. But the Spaniards' greed grew as the loot piled up in the treasure room. *"Oro! Más oro!"* soldiers demanded, "Gold! More gold!" Rumor said that Atahuallpa was deliberately stalling to gain time to plan an escape and to mass armies for a surprise attack. He was quick to point out that these charges made no sense. After all, he was Pizarro's prisoner, not the other way around. Why should he start trouble, when he'd be the first to suffer? If the ransom seemed to be coming in slowly, he said, it was because it had to be carried on men's backs over great distances. If Pizarro didn't believe this, let him see for himself. Let him send patrols to search the country-

Bringing Atahuallpa's ransom as pictured by Théodore de Bry. Although the Indians dressed differently than shown here, the sizes of the pieces of gold and silver they brought are quite accurate.

side around Cajamarca and men to supervise the collection of gold in Cuzco. All would travel under the personal protection of the Sapa Inca.

Pizarro accepted the invitations. On January 5, 1533, his brother Hernando led twenty cavalry and seventeen infantry south to Huamachuco, where the armies were supposedly massing. Finding nothing, he went on to Pachacamac, in the coastal desert south of modern Lima.

One of the most sacred places in the Incan world, Pachacamac was said to be as wealthy as Cuzco. The moment Hernando arrived, he headed for the temple that stood on a hilltop overlooking the Pacific. He wasn't welcome. Priests met him at the main gate, barring the way. The temple, they insisted, was so sacred that only the Sapa Inca and certain holy men might enter, and then only after fasting and prayer.

Hernando just scowled and brushed past them, followed by his men with swords drawn. But as they strode up the hillside, a minor earthquake shook the ground. The priests shrank back, expecting the earth to open and swallow the intruders. The Spaniards, however, saw the tremor as a divine order to strike the devil in his den.

The Spaniards were disappointed when they burst into the temple. Instead of a hall paneled with gold, they found a tiny, darkened chamber. In the darkest corner stood a wooden idol with a man's face and a monster's body. The idol was crusted with dried blood and stank of countless sacrifices. Cursing and grimacing, Hernando's men hauled it into the sunlight and smashed it to bits in front of the priests. After a speech on the sin of idol worship, Hernando had "the devil's chamber" cleaned and set up a large cross. The priests bowed, for the strangers' huaca had proven itself mightier than their gods'.

Unfortunately, the fabled treasures of Pachacamac had vanished. When the priests heard that Atahuallpa was collecting ransom, they stripped the temple; they'd been loyal to Huáscar and would do nothing to help his murderer. Hernando, furious, tortured an old priest to make him reveal the treasure's location. A knotted rope was tied around the priest's forehead and twisted until it seemed that his eyes would pop out. The poor man led them to several hundred pounds of gold buried near the temple, a good haul, if only a drop in the bucket. According to Inca legend, the real treasure was buried in the coastal desert, where it still waits to be uncovered.

Hernando's disappointment turned to joy when he heard that an equally valuable prize was nearby. General Chalcuchima, conqueror of Cuzco, was at Jauja, one hundred fifty miles to the east, with an army of thirty-five thousand. Although he had only thirty-seven men, Hernando decided to go to Jauja. His decision, reckless as it may seem, was actually well thought out. By then, the Spaniards had learned a good deal about how the Inca system worked. They understood that the Sapa Inca's governors and generals might run the empire on a daily basis, but they could not make important decisions. That was too bad, because Chalcuchima might have seized Hernando and held him hostage for his master. But orders were orders; he wouldn't dare harm anyone under Atahuallpa's protection.

The road to Jauja passed over some of the most rugged country in the Andes. The conquistadores climbed steep passes and crossed swaying bridges. It was so rough that the horses' shoes wore out. And, since there was no iron, new shoes were forged in pure silver. Seldom have invaders traveled in such style.

Chalcuchima met Hernando's force in the plaza of Jauja. There were to be no surprises this time. The square was lined with warriors, ready to spring at any wrong move. Standing nearby were spearmen displaying pieces of those who'd defied the Sapa Inca's general. Pedro Pizarro was astonished at such cruelty, although Spanish cruelty seems not to have bothered him. Although Chalcuchima said he'd come in peace, "He held ready in the plaza of Jauja many lances, and on the points of some were placed heads of Indians, and on others tongues, and on others hands, so that it was a fearful thing to see the cruelties which he had committed and was committing."

Hernando decided to try "sweet talk" (his words) instead of force. Like his brother Francisco, he was a master of the clever lie. He told Chalcuchima that the Sapa Inca had ordered him to leave his army and return with the Spaniards to Cajamarca. The general had no choice but to obey. He set off with Hernando, accompanied by hundreds of servants and a string of llamas carrying Jauja's share of the ransom.

The moment they arrived at Cajamarca, Chalcuchima paid his respects to his master. The Spaniards were impressed by the way the Inca's greatest general appeared before his commander-

113

in-chief. He entered Atahuallpa's room barefoot, with a load on his back. Seeing Atahuallpa, he raised his hands to the sun to give thanks for being allowed to see him again. Slowly, meekly, he went up to Atahuallpa and kissed his face, hands, and feet. Then he broke down. With tears rolling down his cheeks, he said that the Son of the Sun would never have been taken had he, Chalcuchima, been at Cajamarca with his warriors. Atahuallpa, dignified as ever, neither looked him in the face nor showed the slightest emotion. Chalcuchima was later tortured with fire to make him surrender hidden treasure. By the time the Spaniards realized that he had nothing to give, they'd crippled his legs.

Hernando returned with Chalcuchima on April 25, 1533, after a three-month absence. Diego de Almagro had arrived only eleven days earlier with one hundred fifty infantry and fifty cavalry, more than doubling the Spanish force. Treasure, too, was arriving. What had been a trickle early in the year was now a flood. Thousands of pesos of gold and silver came to the treasure rooms each day.* The richest booty was from the Temple of the Sun in Cuzco. Shortly after Hernando left, three soldiers had been sent there to hasten gold shipments. These three were thugs of the worst kind. Traveling under the Sapa Inca's safe-conduct, they did whatever they pleased. The Indians' feelings meant nothing to them, nor did their beliefs, which they damned as devil worship. They broke into Cuzco's House of the Chosen Women to rape some of the inmates. They invaded the sacred precincts of the coricancha and, as priests hid their eyes with their cloaks, pried golden slabs off the walls with copper crowbars. Only Atahuallpa's safe-conduct prevented General Quizquiz, commanding the army of occupation, from treating them as they deserved. But they did their job admirably, sending a vast treasure to Cajamarca, although it was only a fraction of what they'd left behind.

---

*The peso was both a Spanish coin and a unit of weight; that is, one-hundredth of a pound.

Spanish bookkeepers had their work cut out for them, cataloging the treasure as it arrived. Pedro Sancho, Pizarro's secretary, described part of it in his *An Account of the Conquest of Peru,* 1543:

> *[The treasure included] five hundred odd plates of gold torn from some house walls in Cuzco; and even the smallest plates weighed four or five pounds apiece; other, larger ones, weighed ten or twelve pounds, and with plates of this sort the walls of that temple were covered. They also brought a seat of very fine gold, worked into the form of a footstool, which weighed eighteen thousand pesos. Likewise they brought a fountain all of gold and very subtilely worked which was very fair to see as much for the skill of the work as for the shape which it has been given; and there were many other pieces such as vases, jars, and plates which they also brought.*

By June 1533, it was time to distribute the treasure. Pizarro had nine furnaces built and set Indian smiths to melting the metal into bars of standard size and weight. Everything went into the furnaces, except a few exceptional items sent to Spain as examples of Peruvian art. These items included a golden ear of maize encased in silver leaves, golden spiders and hummingbirds, and a life-size boy cast in solid gold. King Charles, however, was uninterested in this type of art. After putting the items on display for a couple of weeks, he had them melted down and minted into coins. Not one survived, and the world lost some of the most precious works of human genius.

When the smiths completed their task a month later, Pizarro had 13,420 pounds of "good gold" and 26,000 pounds of silver. By any standard of measurement, this was a fantastic haul. Today, with gold valued at about $450 an ounce, Pizarro's gold bars would be worth $96,624,000. His silver bars, with silver valued at $7.70 an ounce, would fetch $3,203,200. The grand total would be

$101,759,680, making Atahuallpa's ransom the largest in history.

The treasure was not distributed equally, but according to rank. First came King Charles, whose "king's fifth" was immediately set aside and marked with the royal emblem. The remainder was then divided so that one share equaled forty-five pounds of gold and ninety pounds of silver. Francisco Pizarro took the most, thirteen shares ($4,440,384), plus Atahuallpa's golden throne, weighing 183 pounds ($1,343,952). None could deny that he'd become a "son of someone." Hernando Pizarro received seven shares ($2,390,976), Hernando de Soto four shares ($1,366,272). The common soldiers were also handsomely rewarded. Each cavalryman was given two shares ($683,136) and each foot soldier one share ($341,568). The true value of money, however, depends upon what it can buy. And in 1533 it bought a lot. A skilled Spanish craftsman could support his family comfortably on fifty dollars a year; a peasant farmer could get by on half that sum. Even the humblest of the Men of Cajamarca were set for life, provided they went home quickly enough. Few did.

Almost immediately, their wealth began to slip through their fingers. With so much treasure in circulation, prices skyrocketed. Even small items began to cost many times more than in Spain. Horses were a "bargain" at 2,500 gold pesos. A bottle of wine cost sixty pesos, a sword seventy pesos, and a sheet of paper ten pesos. Even a string of garlic brought half a peso. Yet the Spaniards were so rich that they lost all sense of proportion. They spent freely, and gambled even more freely. If a man owed another, he paid with a lump of gold, without weighing it or caring if it was worth twice the amount of the debt. Peru was a rich land, and there would always be more loot, they thought.

The newcomers, however, fared poorly. According to their agreement, Pizarro and his partners were to divide the spoils equally. Father Luque, having died after the expedition sailed, forfeited his share. And now Pizarro changed the rules for his other partner, Diego de Almagro. Since Almagro hadn't helped

116

with Atahuallpa's capture, he wasn't entitled to equal shares of the ransom, said Pizarro. But, as he was a "generous" man, he gave Almagro a hundred thousand pesos. Almagro's men received a hundred pesos each and a promise. When they took Cuzco, with its richer treasures, they'd share equally in all of the loot.

What about Atahuallpa? He'd paid the ransom and was entitled to his freedom.

Pizarro agreed. He even prepared an announcement saying that Atahuallpa had kept his bargain and should be released, except for one problem. Since the Spaniards were few and surrounded by enemies, it would be unwise to let him go immediately. What Pizarro was really saying was that it would *never* be wise to release him.

Atahuallpa had outlived his usefulness and now stood in the Spaniards' way. Everyone wanted to go on to Cuzco, especially

Atahuallpa guarded by a Spanish soldier after his capture at Cajamarca. His capture paralyzed the Inca, who'd been taught never to think for themselves, but to act only on orders of the Sapa Inca. Atahuallpa's captors treated him with respect until shortly before his execution, when they put him in chains.

117

Almagro's men, who had yet to make their fortunes. Atahuallpa's death guaranteed to them that any future treasure would not be part of his ransom. "In that case," they argued, "let us kill Atahuallpa right away; nobody will be the loser, and everything we get later we shall have earned together, so that they can no longer deny us our share!"

Pizarro had other, equally strong, reasons for doing away with his prisoner. It is doubtful if he ever meant to keep his part of the bargain. He realized that once Atahuallpa was free he'd be a rallying point for Inca resistance. A long march over difficult country lay ahead. However closely Atahuallpa was guarded, there would be hundreds of opportunities for him to escape. Worse, his presence with the column would encourage rescue efforts. The proud ruler hadn't forgotten his humiliation at Cajamarca. If he ever got his hands on the Spaniards, they'd wind up like Huáscar's followers. Contract or no contract, the Sapa Inca couldn't leave Cajamarca alive. True, his death would be murder, albeit a "necessary murder" in Pizarro's eyes.

Once again rumors flew about the Spanish camp. Atahuallpa had massed two hundred thousand men at Huamachuco, among them thirty thousand cannibals! They were preparing to march on Cajamarca! It is unclear how these rumors began, but they spread like wildfire. Some modern students believe they were planted by Pizarro as an excuse for the murder he'd planned.

What followed was a deadly serious farce. One day, Pizarro accused Atahuallpa of treachery. "I have treated you as a brother," he said. "Why this treason?" He had invaded Atahuallpa's realm, butchered his nobles, and held him at ransom— all "as a brother."

The Sapa Inca was dumbfounded. "Are you joking?" he cried. "You are always telling me jokes. What chance would I or all my men have of disturbing men as brave as you? Stop mocking me like this."

To prove how serious he was, Pizarro had a heavy chain put around the Sapa Inca's neck. Events now moved swiftly. Her-

118

nando de Soto was against harming the prisoner. If he was suspected of a crime, de Soto wanted him sent to Spain for trial. Since de Soto was popular among the officers and might cause trouble, Pizarro decided to send him on a wild-goose chase. He sent him to investigate Huamachuco. Hernando Pizarro, whom Atahuallpa trusted, had already left for Spain with the king's share of the booty; a journey, as we shall see, that would have important consequences.

On July 26, 1533, Atahuallpa went on trial for his life. There were five main charges against him, each more ridiculous than the other. He was charged, first, with plotting treason against the invaders; that is, wanting to regain what they'd stolen. The other charges were idol worship, having many wives, incest, and lavishing public property on his relatives and friends. In short, the Sapa Inca was accused of acting like an Inca, according to the laws and customs of his people.

His trial—if that is the proper word for it—was rigged. Atahuallpa had none of the rights taken for granted in Spain at that time. He could not call witnesses in his defense or question the evidence against him. He wasn't even present at the trial, being kept chained in another room. Pizarro, Almagro, and Friar Valverde were at once his accusers, his judges, and his jury. Their verdict was a foregone conclusion: guilty as charged; his sentence, to be burned alive.

Pizarro brought him the sentence in person. Now, for the first time, Atahuallpa showed emotion. That was the worst death a Sapa Inca could suffer. Burning meant that he couldn't be mummified, couldn't return to his father the Sun. He'd dealt honestly with the Spaniards, he pleaded, his eyes filling with tears. If they wanted more gold, he'd double, no, triple, the ransom. He'd pay anything, do anything, to avoid the flames. Pizarro only repeated the sentence and left the room.

It was night when they took Atahuallpa for execution. Torchbearers lit the way as the procession filed into the plaza of Cajamarca, that place of evil memory. The plaza was crowded with

119

Indians. All lay on the ground, face down, weeping and moaning as he passed, but not daring to look at him.

In the center of the plaza stood a wooden stake surrounded by bundles of brushwood. Passing through a ring of soldiers, Atahuallpa was led to the stake. All around him, their faces lit by flickering torches, were enemies who were as cruel to him as he'd been to Huáscar. Atahuallpa trembled, but not from the cold night air.

Suddenly a man stood before him. Friar Valverde had come to make him an offer. If Atahuallpa abandoned his false gods and became a Christian, he'd be strangled instead of burned. Atahuallpa nodded agreement. Valverde then baptised him and christened him Juan de Atahuallpa. His work finished, the priest made way for the executioner. "Care for my children!" the condemned man called to Pizarro as the executioner stepped forward.

This man, whoever he was, knew his job. He sat Atahuallpa on a stool, tied him to the stake, and slipped a rope around his neck. He then passed a stick through the loop and twisted. Slowly, his eyes bulging and face turning purple, the Son of the Sun died. The body was left at the stake during the night, guarded by soldiers.

De Soto returned that same night. Upon learning of the execution, he became furious with Pizarro. "You have done an evil thing," cried one of de Soto's men who shared his anger. "You should have awaited our return. There is not a single warrior in the country, and we have received friendly treatment everywhere."

Atahuallpa received Christian burial in the morning. Pizarro and his fellow murderers sat through the service, shedding crocodile tears. Suddenly, the service was interrupted by the shrieks of Atahuallpa's sister-wives. They burst in, demanding that his grave be enlarged, for they intended to follow their lord into the next world. After being told that he'd died a Christian and no longer belonged to them, they returned to their quarters, where several hanged themselves.

Atahuallpa was buried alongside some Spanish soldiers who'd died of disease, although he wasn't to stay there long. A few nights later, Indians stole his body and took it to Quito for mummification.

Early in August 1533, Pizarro had one of Atahuallpa's brothers, Tupac Huallpa, crowned Sapa Inca. An easygoing man, he seemed an ideal puppet who'd do as he was told. The Spaniards left Cajamarca to complete the conquest of Peru.

4

CONQUEST AND REBELLION

THE DEATH OF ATAHUALLPA BROKE THE SPELL THE Indians had been under since his capture. The armies of Quito had pledged their loyalty to him, not to the feeble puppet, Tupac Huallpa. With Atahuallpa gone, they were free to resist his murderers. Strong and undefeated, they still controlled much of Peru. The army Chalcuchima had led held the road to Cuzco; Quizquiz waited with his army outside the capital. If Pizarro wanted to conquer the entire country, he'd have to fight.

The Spaniards traveled the road to Cuzco for two months without opposition. They were never alone. Bands of warriors appeared constantly on hilltops overlooking the route. The warriors would watch for a while, then disappear, only to reappear later.

Outside Jauja, where Hernando Pizarro had sweet-talked Chalcuchima, they made their move. A wide, shallow river crossed the valley in front of the city. On the other side Chalcuchima's men stood in battle array. Calmly they waited to destroy the strangers and free their general.

The conquistadores, however, had other plans. Although

122

outnumbered a hundred to one, they spurred their horses and went right for the Indians. That was the Spanish way, learned on countless European battlefields. When outnumbered, they'd cross themselves, say a quick prayer, and charge. The tactic usually worked; for the enemy, startled by their boldness, fled before these wildmen.

That's what happened outside Jauja. For the first time since landing in Peru seventeen months before, the Spaniards went into action against an armed enemy. As falconets boomed and cross-bow arrows whizzed through the air, a hundred horsemen splashed into the river, shouting "Santiago, and at them!" The Indian front collapsed, each man fleeing in panic.

Jauja was the capital of the Huanca tribe, conquered during the early years of Inca expansion. The Huanca hated their over-lords, who'd treated them with brutality. Chalcuchima's occupa-tion had only deepened their hatred of the Inca—all Inca. The Spaniards were their liberators, and they welcomed them when they rode into town. Jauja was such a pleasant spot that Pizarro decided to rest there while Hernando de Soto went ahead with sixty horsemen to scout the route to Cuzco.

It was during this scouting mission that the conquistadores discovered how well the Inca could fight. Late one afternoon, de Soto came to the canyon of the Apurímac, "The Great Speaker," River. The Apurímac deserved its name, because, when in flood, it "spoke" with the roar of the Earthquake and Thunder gods. Since the bridge over the canyon had been burned, the Spaniards had to ford the river. Fortunately, it was November, the driest time of the year in the Andes. Nevertheless, it was hard going across the slippery stones and the rushing waters that came up to the horses' chests.

Once across the Apurímac, the Spaniards entered a narrow gorge with steep cliffs on either side. The crossing had tired both men and horses; the climb in the afternoon heat exhausted them. But since no Indians had been seen for days, they felt secure.

INCA AND SPANIARD

They'd stopped to rest when, suddenly, bloodcurdling screams pierced the air. Thousands of Inca swooped down the cliffs, determined to wipe them out. De Soto cried, "Santiago!" but the road was too narrow to mount a charge. Sling stones bounced off armor. Warriors surged around the horses, grabbing their tails, holding their legs, overturning them in a cloud of dust and flailing hooves. Hands reached up, dragging Spaniards to the ground. These immediately had their heads split open by clubs and maces. At last the Inca were fighting on their own terms—hand-to-hand.

De Soto's men were not fighting for victory, but for their lives. Panting, rivulets of sweat running down their dust-covered faces, they lashed out with sword and spur. Swords sliced through wooden helmets, shattering the skulls inside them. Spurs became bloody as riders urged their mounts forward, until at last they broke through to level ground atop a low hill, where they camped within sight of the enemy.

The Inca jeered and held up gory trophies. Five Spaniards had been killed when toppled from their horses; their heads were now held high on spears. Warriors waved horses' tails and proudly displayed horses' heads.

De Soto posted sentries and had his men turn in for the night. Few slept, fearing attack at any moment. Yet there was no need for fear. The Inca, they'd learn, rarely fought at night.

It was past midnight when a beautiful sound echoed in the canyon below. It was the call of a bugle. Pizarro, fearing just such an ambush, had sent Almagro to reinforce the scouting party with another thirty horsemen. No sooner did de Soto hear the call, than he had his own bugler answer.

At daybreak the Indians expected to see de Soto's men cowering on the hill. What they saw were Spaniards formed in line-of-battle: eighty-five horsemen in a single line, stirrup to stirrup, with swords raised before them. The Indians ran away; anyone unable to run fast enough died under the swinging blades.

Altogether, the Spaniards would fight four battles on the road to Cuzco. Each battle, although differing from the others in detail, always ended in victory for the conquistadores. Although Spanish courage played a vital role each time, their courage would have been useless without horses. The Indians never had a chance against the Spaniards on flat ground. After a while even the largest Indian force was looked upon with contempt. "I took no more notice of a hundred armed Indians than I would have of a handful of flies," said one soldier. An arrogant boast surely, but true nevertheless.

Meantime, back at Jauja, Pizarro was in a sour mood. Tupac Huallpa had died of an illness that looked like poisoning. Chalcuchima was suspected of murdering him, although there was no proof. When Pizarro learned of the ambush at the Apurímac gorge, he decided that the general was secretly plotting against the Spaniards. He had Chalcuchima put in chains and made him a promise: "You can rest assured that . . . as soon as I arrive where Captain [de Soto] is waiting with my men, I shall have you burned alive." He was as good as his word.

On November 13, 1533, the Spaniards joined forces at the pass above Cuzco. Chalcuchima was tied to a stake, while Friar Valverde tried to persuade him to imitate his master with a last-minute conversion to Christianity. But the general was made of sterner stuff. He declared that he understood neither the white man nor his religion. As the flames leaped up before him, he called upon the Inca gods and General Quizquiz to avenge his death.

Chalcuchima's ashes were still warm when a young Indian strode into the Spanish camp accompanied by several orejones. Coolly, he explained that he was Manco, a younger brother of Huáscar's. By some miracle he'd escaped Atahuallpa's butchers and hidden in the mountains. Now he'd come to claim his rightful place as Sapa Inca.

Pizarro, delighted, made a flowery speech. He assured Manco that he'd come for no other reason than to help him in any way he could. Reporting the speech, Pedro Sancho added, ". . . the Governor made him all these promises solely in order to please him."

On Saturday, November 15, 1533, exactly a year after arriving at Cajamarca, the Spaniards entered Cuzco. They marched two abreast along narrow streets toward Joy Square. They marched wide-eyed and openmouthed, astonished at the Inca capital. Nothing like it existed in Europe. Despite the looting of the three soldiers months earlier, the city glinted with gold. Its walls were so well made that it was difficult to push the blade of a knife between the massive stones. "This city is the greatest and finest ever seen in this country or anywhere in the Indies," a soldier wrote home. "[It] is so beautiful and has such fine buildings that it would be remarkable even in Spain." Watching over it from a mountaintop to the north was the fortress of Sacsahuamán, a gray mass of stone that seemed to have been thrust up through the earth by the gods themselves.

Manco's coronation was a splendid spectacle. For thirty days Cuzco celebrated, sometimes with dignity, at other times crudely. The royal mummies were paraded to the sound of solemn music and chanting. This was followed by drinking chicha and dancing until everyone collapsed from exhaustion and happiness. A soldier named Miguel de Estete described the scene:

> So vast a number of people assembled every day that they could only crowd the square with difficulty. Manco had all the dead ancestors brought to the festivities. . . . They were . . . brought into the city seated on their thrones in order of precedence. There was a litter for each one, with men in its livery to carry it. . . . A pavilion was erected for each of them, and the dead [kings] were placed in these in order, seated on their thrones and surrounded by pages and women with flywhisks in their hands, who ministered to them with as much respect as if they had been alive. . . .

126

Manco on his throne surrounded by orejones, "big ears." Since Pizarro had killed Manco's enemy, Atahuallpa, Manco thought Pizarro a friend and welcomed him. Pizarro, thinking he'd made a useful puppet, had Manco crowned Sapa Inca. Both were wrong.

There were so many people, and both men and women were such heavy drinkers . . . that it is a fact that two wide drains over [eighteen inches] in diameter . . . ran with urine throughout the day from those who urinated into them, as abundantly as a flowing spring. This was not remarkable when one considers the amount they were drinking and the numbers drinking it. But the sight was a marvel and something never seen before.

Yet the Inca couldn't help noticing who was in control. Although Manco was the Son of the Sun, he had to swear allegiance to King Charles and his servant Francisco Pizarro.

The Spaniards quickly wore out their welcome. The coronation over, they went on a rampage. Soldiers tore the golden ornaments from the royal mummies and broke open tombs to rob the dead. Private homes were raided in the search for treasure. In one house Pedro Pizarro found ten slabs of the purest silver, each twenty feet long by a foot wide and three fingers thick. His comrades discovered golden statues of women and llamas, life-size, plus countless golden jars, pitchers, and other items. They strode into the coricancha as if it was theirs to do with as they pleased. When challenged by the Villac Umu, the high priest, they pushed him aside. Works of art were smashed to get at their precious metals. Beautiful things were destroyed just for the pleasure of ruining something others cherished. A rough list of the loot filled ninety closely written pages.

Not all Spaniards, however, approved of this rampage. Father Cristóbal de Molina, an army chaplain, condemned his comrades' greed and ignorance. "Their only concern was to collect gold and silver to make themselves rich . . . without thinking that they were doing wrong and were wrecking and destroying. For what was being destroyed was more perfect than anything they enjoyed and possessed."

Although they collected more treasure at Cuzco than at Cajamarca, a much larger amount was lost. The people of Cuzco, like those of Pachacamac, despised Atahuallpa. When chasquis brought Atahuallpa's ransom demands, the orejones hid whatever could be removed from the city.

Gold and silver were carried out on the backs of warriors. Arriving near the hiding place, all were dismissed, except for the fifty or one hundred men needed to finish the job. These moved the treasure to the selected spot and buried it. The warriors were then marched far away and ordered to hang themselves. Finally

128

the orejones who'd directed the operation committed suicide, taking the secret of the hiding place with them to the grave. Despite the efforts of searchers during the next four centuries, most of Cuzco's treasure has never been recovered.

Pizarro, meantime, was using Cuzco as a base for mopping-up operations. By now Manco knew the kind of people the strangers were. Yet he helped them on the principle that "the enemy of my enemy is my friend." He meant to use the Spaniards to settle scores with the men of Quito. But beyond that, we can't say what he intended to do about his "friends."

When Quizquiz attacked Jauja, Manco led an Indian army to the rescue. Spearheaded by Almagro's cavalry, Manco's army slowly pushed Quizquiz northward. Quizquiz's captains, discouraged by their defeats, begged their general to make peace. When he refused, calling them cowards, they killed him and the army melted away.

Only one of Atahuallpa's generals still remained in the field. Rumiñaui, "Stone-Eye," had led his men to Quito after the massacre at Cajamarca. Pizarro decided to finish him off with a double blow. He sent Almagro and Sebastián de Benalcázar, a trusted captain, north with two separate forces. Benalcázar reached Rumiñaui's forces first.

On May 3, 1534, the two armies fought the greatest battle of the conquest at Teocajas, south of Quito. It seemed at first that the Indians couldn't help winning. Rumiñaui had fifty thousand men to his enemy's one hundred forty. But Teocajas was a plain, and Benalcázar's men were mounted. That made all the difference.

"Santiago, and at them!"

Three times the Indians were met by horsemen who cut through their ranks with swords and lances. Clever as the Indians were, they couldn't find a way to combat this method of attack. They tried building traps to bring down the horses. Pits were dug, planted with sharp stakes at the bottom, and covered with branches and earth. Holes the size of a horse's hoof were also dug in the ground. But the Spaniards were wise to such tricks, which had been used in Europe for centuries. Only four horses and as many riders were killed that day, compared to two thousand Indian dead and wounded. Teocajas proved that no amount of Indian courage could beat the Spaniards in the open.

Quito fell on June 22, 1534. Yet there was nothing left for its conquerors to enjoy. Rather than leave the city to them, Rumiñaui had turned it into a mass of smoking, tumbled-down rubble; even Atahuallpa's mummy was destroyed and the pieces scattered. Rumiñaui's fate is unknown. He retreated into the Eastern Cordillera, never to be seen again.

The fall of Quito made Pizarro master of Peru. No longer a conqueror, he had to become a governor. The first step in governing was to select a site for a capital. Cuzco, although Peru's greatest city, was too far inland. The sea was Pizarro's lifeline to the outside world. Everything needed for the colony's survival— soldiers, supplies, munitions—had to come by water.

On January 6, 1535, Pizarro founded El Ciudad de los Reyes, "The City of the Kings," honoring the three kings who'd visited the baby Jesus. Indians were set to work laying out the streets and main square, fronted by a cathedral, governor's palace, and other official buildings. The city was built at the mouth of a river whose Indian name, Rimac, the Spaniard's pronounced "Lima." Both river and city were soon to be known by that name.

Pizarro was mistaken if he thought he'd enjoy his conquest in peace. While busy with the building of Lima, he named Almagro military governor of Cuzco. Almagro, however, had grander notions of his place in the world. On the day he took up his command, he met with a friend just back from a secret mission. Distrusting the Pizarros, Almagro had feared they would doublecross him, as Francisco had already done several times. When Hernando Pizarro had left for Spain, Almagro had sent this friend to report on Hernando's activities. That friend, whose name is unknown, returned several months ahead of Hernando with important news.

Hernando Pizarro had reached Spain in January 1534 and had been welcomed with open arms. King Charles, desperate for money, was overjoyed with his share of the Peruvian treasure. In gratitude, he rewarded all the leaders of the expedition with titles and offices. Hernando was made Knight of Santiago and Valverde became Bishop of Cuzco. Francisco Pizarro joined the Spanish nobility with the title Marquis of Atavillos; henceforth he'd be known simply as the Marquis. As governor of New Castile, he was assigned a territory extending roughly eight hundred miles to the south of Puna Island. Almagro was to have his own territory, New Toledo, present-day Chile, extending six hundred miles beyond Pizarro's lands. Unfortunately, there were as yet no maps of South America and the king hadn't the slightest idea of what he was giving away.

As soon as Almagro heard the news, he claimed Cuzco as part of his domain. The Marquis said it belonged to him. Each had his supporters, who'd have killed one another had the leaders not patched up their differences—again. They agreed to make no decision about Cuzco until Hernando arrived with King Charles's actual orders. In the meantime, Almagro would explore Chile.

Everyone expected Chile to be another golden land. Adventurers, who'd been pouring into Peru for months, rushed to join the expedition. Hernando de Soto asked to be its second-in-command, but was refused. He returned to Spain with a fortune and received a royal license to explore Florida. As soon as Almagro left for Chile, July 1535, the Marquis put his brothers Juan and Gonzalo in command of Cuzco. It was a decision he'd bitterly regret.

The younger Pizarros couldn't govern themselves, let alone a large city. To their greed for gold was added a viciousness that would have brought swift punishment in Spain. They put themselves above the law; indeed, they became a law unto themselves. Not content to loot, they turned their troops loose on the people

su hija su f ysuma
Due los pobres yns

Seeds of revolt. The Spaniards were not gentle as conquerors. Here one steals a girl while her parents look on, helpless to protect her. Such behavior made the Spaniards both hated and feared.

of Cuzco. People were insulted, tortured, and murdered. Orejones were thrown into the street and their houses taken by Spaniards. Soldiers raided the Houses of the Chosen Women to rape their inmates. If a soldier fancied a woman, he took her. If her husband or father protested, a sword shut him up. The Inca were becoming slaves in their own land.

The Sapa Inca suffered as much as any of his subjects. Soldiers raped his wives before his eyes, and the Pizarros chuckled; Manco was only an Indian and his feelings counted for nothing. More, Gonzalo took a liking to the lovely Cura Ocllo, Manco's full sister and his favorite wife.

Manco was stunned when he learned of this. Knowing the Spaniard's greed, he tried to satisfy him with silver.

Gonzalo wanted more.

"Well, señor Manco Inca," he snarled, "let's have the lady. . . . All this silver is fine, but she is what we really want." And with those words, he dragged her to his quarters.

Hatred burned in Manco's heart, and he vowed to destroy those he'd once helped. His advisors agreed. The Inca nation was at stake, and unless something was done soon, it would be crushed. "We cannot spend our entire lives in such great misery and subjection. Let us rebel once and for all. Let us die for our liberty, and for the wives and children whom they continually take from us and abuse."

One night in October 1535, Manco explained his plans at a secret meeting of orejones. With Almagro gone, the Spaniards held Cuzco with a mere handful of soldiers. The time had come to strike! Manco must escape and rally the people for a war of liberation.

That night, Manco slipped out of Cuzco in his litter. But luck was against him. His absence was quickly discovered, and Gonzalo Pizarro went in pursuit with a troop of cavalry. They caught up with the royal party a few miles outside the city and Manco was brought back under armed guard.

The Pizarros, furious, tormented him as never before. They locked him in a dungeon, chained to the wall hand and foot. Officers called him "dog," spat on him, and burned his eyelashes with candles. Guards slapped him, poured filth over him, and used his nose as a candle snuffer. Sometimes they kept him with a chain around his neck in the street for all to see. We know of these abuses from the Spaniards themselves, who wrote about them freely. Manco also told his sons about them years later.

Hernando Pizarro returned in January 1536 and took over the command of Cuzco. A prudent man, he released Manco and tried to patch things up with him. But it was too late. The Sapa Inca wanted no Spaniard's friendship. He wanted only Spanish blood.

Manco began to fight the strangers with their own weapons, with cunning and deceit. Claiming that certain orejones were needed elsewhere, he got permission for them to leave Cuzco. They really were needed, but not in the way he'd led Hernando to believe. Once free, the orejones began planning a great rebellion. With Incan thoroughness, they made sure of every detail. Chasquis sped across the Land of the Four Quarters to call the people to arms. Traveling by night, warriors converged on Cuzco, keeping under cover until Manco could lead them. Those who stayed behind planted extra crops, should the campaign last longer than expected.

Slowly, carefully, Manco won Hernando's trust by playing on his greed. That wasn't hard to do. To show his "gratitude" for having been released, from time to time Manco told where treasure was buried. It was always there, and Hernando congratulated himself that he, at least, knew how to get along with Indians.

Manco made his move during Easter 1536. He asked permission to leave Cuzco for a few days to offer prayers at a certain huaca in the country. That huaca, he added, smiling, was near one of the greatest treasures of all, a life-size statue of his father, Huayna Capac, in solid gold. He wanted Hernando to have it as a token of his appreciation, he said. The only problem was that the statue lay hidden in a cave in the mountains. Lookouts always watched the cave and, at the first sign of Spaniards, they would move it elsewhere.

Hernando snapped up the golden bait. Manco could go for the statue, guarded by only two soldiers. And, since the Sapa Inca

134

must always travel in style, his favorite wives and orejones could go along. He seemed like such a tame puppet that Hernando thought him incapable of trickery.

Manco left Cuzco on April 18, 1536. It was his turn to laugh.

The Sapa Inca stood in a secluded valley north of Cuzco. On either side of him was a giant golden vessel of chicha. The valley before him and the surrounding hillsides swarmed with warriors. Feather capes and headdresses flashed with pinpoints of colored light. Copper spear points and battle-axes glistened in the sun. The warriors sat silently, intently, waiting.

Manco nodded and the high priest of the Sun stepped forward. In a booming voice he found words for what everyone felt in his heart. The strangers were devils. The strangers meant to crush the Inca. The strangers must be exterminated.

He finished and the chicha vessels were uncovered. Manco drank first, crying: "This is a pledge that we shall kill them all—all, and leave not one alive!" For the rest of that day, and throughout the night, the valley echoed to Inca war songs and war dances. Each warrior promised himself that, one day soon, he'd drink chicha from a Spanish skull and beat on a Spanish man-drum.

A week passed before Hernando realized that he'd been tricked. Then, swearing vengeance, he sent his brother Juan with sixty cavalrymen to bring Manco back.

Juan and his troopers found the area around Cuzco strangely quiet. Village after village was empty, except for women, children, and old men. Men of fighting age were nowhere to be seen.

They learned the reason when they met the two soldiers who'd been escorting Manco. They were lucky to be alive, they said. Manco had let them go as messengers to tell the Spaniards that he'd soon return to Cuzco at the head of an army. Let the white men say their prayers, for they hadn't long to live.

Now Juan Pizarro was many things—liar, bully, killer. But he was no coward. Showing his back to the enemy would dishonor the Pizarro name, and he couldn't do that for the world. Rather than retreat, he pushed on, determined to get Manco even if he had to cut through an army to do it.

He had his chance at the Yucay River. Thousands of battle-ready Indians were massed on its eastern bank, daring him to attack. Without hesitating, he had the bugler sound the call.

For the next three days the Spaniards drove the Indians before them. Again and again the Spaniards charged, breaking the Indian front and leaving behind a trail of dead and dying. But the Indians refused to give ground. They always rallied, renewing the battle.

Juan had already lost several men and horses when a messenger arrived from his brother Hernando. Indians were massing around Cuzco. He must return before the trap closed.

Returning to Cuzco, the horsemen saw an awesome sight. Indians were everywhere, camped on the plain and the heights above the city. With nowhere to go except straight ahead, the riders closed ranks and charged. To their surprise, the Indians allowed them to pass, possibly because the Indians hoped to destroy their enemy all at once. That was their first mistake, and would cost them dearly.

The Men of Cajamarca were used to being outnumbered, but this was different. Never had they faced an Inca army led by a Son of the Sun in person. Pedro Pizarro recalled that his comrades didn't sleep that night: "So numerous were the [Indian] troops who came here that they covered the fields, and by day it looked as if a black cloth had been spread over the ground for half a league (about two miles) around this city of Cuzco. At night there were so many fires that it looked like nothing other than a very serene sky full of stars. There was so much shouting and din of voices that all of us were astonished. When all the [Inca warriors] arrived, it was understood . . . that there were two hundred thousand of them who had come to lay siege [to Cuzco]." Even if Pedro exaggerated by half, a hundred thousand was still many more than the two hundred Spaniards opposing them. The Spaniards could, however, count on about a thousand Cañari warriors, who had scores to settle with the Inca.

On May 6, 1536, Manco began the siege of Cuzco. Every day for the next eleven months, Spaniard and Inca locked in life-and-death combat.

The siege began with fire. Manco's warrior's heated sling stones red-hot in their camp fires, wrapped them in cotton, and hurled them at Cuzco's thatched roofs. The straw caught fire, and hundreds of buildings were burning before the Spaniards understood how it was being done. Driven by strong winds, the fires leaped from building to building until the whole city was engulfed in flames. Cuzco burned so intensely that Spaniards feared their beards would catch fire at any moment. Finally, all that remained were charred stone walls. Golden Cuzco, sacred city of the Sun, was gone, destroyed by the Inca's own hands. One day a new city, a Spanish city, would rise upon its ruins.

Manco burns Cuzco. In this drawing he is setting fire to a church and the cross inside.

137

INCA AND SPANIARD

Cuzco's defenders, however, were too busy to think about the distant future. They thought in minutes, each of which was a struggle for life. Slowly but surely, Manco's warriors cornered them in a palace at the eastern end of Joy Square. It was death to step outside. Sling stones came with such force and accuracy that a shot to the head could kill a horse. One Spaniard was astonished when a stone hurled from thirty yards away broke his sword in half.

Not that things were much better inside the palace; indeed, they seemed a lot worse. Three times, red-hot sling stones landed on the roof. And three times, they set it ablaze. But just as the Spaniards thought they were goners, the fires went out.

A miracle!

God was on their side!

Several soldiers later claimed that, having lost hope, they looked up and saw the Virgin Mary clad in a blue robe. Descending from the sky, she blew out the fires with her own lips or, said others, doused them with snowflakes. Surely, a doubter jibed, she'd been helped by the Cañari, who'd also fought the flames.

When the fire died out, Hernando set up a defense perimeter around Joy Square. Food was not an immediate problem, nor was water. Yet Manco had them surrounded, and he kept up the pressure. Sling stones and arrows poured in from nearby streets, wounding many although killing few.

Sacsahuamán was especially dangerous. When the siege began, the Indians had easily overpowered the few Spaniards holding the mountaintop fortress. From then on, the Indians had a clear view of everything that went on in the defenders' camp. Slingers and archers bombarded the fortress steadily. An especially nasty Inca practice was to roll down the slope the heads of Spaniards caught outside the city. The fortress became so menacing that it had to be retaken—something more easily said than done.

Sacsahuamán, "The-high-ground-to-attack-which-provides-corpses-for-the-vultures," is the greatest fortress ever built by Native Americans. It is actually a triple ring of terraces, one rising above the other, crowned by three stone towers. Words like "gigantic" and "massive" cannot do it justice. The walls enclosing each terrace are four hundred yards long, rise a total of sixty feet above the ground, and are connected by narrow gateways. Built in zigzags, like the teeth of saws, they are designed for mutual defense. Anyone trying to attack one "tooth" would face rocks dropped from above and sling stones shot from across the way.

The saw-toothed walls of Sacsahuamán as seen from the air. The circular structure in the right background is the foundation of the fortress's main tower. After the Conquest, many of the great stones were used in rebuilding Cuzco, and the fortress's ruins were covered by earth to prevent its use by rebels.

Close-up of the walls of Sacsahuamán. Many of the stones used here weighed over ten tons; the largest weighed over three hundred tons. All were shaped by hand and lifted by human muscle power and rope.

Sacsahuamán's walls are built of stones often 12 feet high and weighing over 10 tons. The largest stone dwarfs any found in the Egyptian pyramids; it is 28 feet tall, 14 feet wide, 12 feet deep, and weighs 361 tons.* Each stone had to be dragged to the site on log rollers, shaped by hand, and hoisted into place by means of ropes and muscle power. Stones often had to be brought from quarries eighteen to twenty miles away. Sometimes even the Inca had to admit defeat, as they did with one monster stone. But they blamed the stone and not themselves for lying down on the job. It is still called *Saycusca,* the "Weary One."

---

*The Epyptian pyramids are built of limestone blocks weighing between 2.5 and 15 tons.

Long after the Conquest, visitors to the fortress couldn't believe that Sacsahuamán was the work of human beings, let alone Indians. The Inca Empire had disappeared and its people, oppressed and ignorant, were not credited with any intelligence at all. Instead, Spaniards claimed the fortress had been built by Satan or by a vanished race of giants. In our own day, some say it is the work of visitors from outer space.

Juan Pizarro was given fifty horsemen and told to take Sacsahuamán. The mission was so dangerous that the Spanish force spent the night before on their knees with hands clasped in prayer. At sunup, they mounted their horses as if to attack some barricades nearby. But instead of attacking there, they charged another barricade, broke through, and galloped up the hillside to the walls of Sacsahuamán.

Things went well—at first. The Inca, unprepared for such a move, had left the first gateway almost unguarded. Dismounting, the Spaniards knocked down part of the gateway and pushed on. Suddenly, as they approached the second gateway, hundreds of Indians began to throw down stones. The stones came thick and fast, forcing the Spaniards back.

Juan, meantime, had remained behind with the mounted men. He'd been wounded in the jaw a day earlier and his head throbbed with pain. It hurt so much that the weight of his helmet and the pressure of its chin strap were unbearable.

Hearing the shouts of his retreating men, he galloped to their aid with the remainder. He went without a helmet, depending on a buckler, a small round shield, to protect him. It didn't. As he neared the second gate, a rock hit him in the head full force. It was a fatal blow. They took the Marquis's younger brother back to Cuzco, where he died in agony.

His comrades spent a cold night near the walls of Sacsahuamán. Although the Inca shouted threats, no attack came. The Spaniards slept—those who could—and tended their wounds. There were no antiseptics or painkillers; coca couldn't be used, for the Spanish priests condemned it as the "devil's herb." Minor wounds were simply bandaged, unwashed, with a strip of rag and left to heal by themselves. Deep cuts were cauterized, closed with a knife blade heated red-hot. A dead Inca might also be cut open for his fat, which was melted and used as an ointment on scrapes and bruises.

Hernando, angered by the setback, vowed to win Sacsahuamán at any cost. As Juan lay dying, Hernando took personal command of the assault. Throughout the following day, while some Spaniards kept the Inca busy at the walls, he had the others make long ladders. After dark he led the entire force up to the walls. Meeting only light resistance, they scaled each wall in turn.

By morning the Inca had retreated to the three towers for a last stand. These towers were behind several buildings filled with Inca warriors. The Spaniards charged repeatedly, only to be driven back each time. It was then that the soldier Hernán Sánchez de Badajoz became a one-man army. He placed a ladder against a building wall, climbed up alone, and squeezed through a window. His sword flashed, Indians screamed, and within minutes he'd cleared the building.

But Hernán Sánchez de Badajoz had only begun to fight. The key to the Indian position was the main tower, which stood nearby, a thick rope dangling from its top. That's all he needed. Crossing himself, he slung his buckler over his back and began to climb the rope hand over hand. Halfway up, a stone "big as a wine jar" glanced harmlessly off his buckler. Once more he squeezed through a window, finding himself in the midst of a group of Inca. Clearing the room, he waved from the window to encourage his comrades to follow.

They did. Ladders went up against all three towers, and soon the Spaniards were fighting their way across the roofs. The Inca commander was the orejon Cahuite, as brave an enemy as the Spaniards had ever met. He carried a captured Spanish sword in one hand and an Inca mace in the other. Pedro Pizarro says he

142

"marched like a lion" from one end of a roof to the other. Whenever a Spaniard showed himself, Cahuite smashed his skull. Any Inca who showed fear was promptly killed and his body thrown into the Spaniards below.

Hernando Pizarro, who respected courage even in an enemy, shouted that this orejon must be taken alive. But for Cahuite life as a captive meant a living death. As the Spaniards began to climb up the towers at several places at once, he flung his weapons in their faces. Then, he stuffed a handful of earth into his mouth, covered his head with his cloak, and jumped from the roof.

Cahuite's death ended Inca resistance. Many, following their chief's example, leaped from the walls. Their bodies lay unburied, a feast for the vultures. The remaining 1,500 prisoners were killed on the spot.

After the capture of Sacsahuamán, the siege of Cuzco became a stalemate. Manco, strong as he was, could not retake his ruined capital. And the Spaniards, few as they were, could not escape from it.

The Inca's religious beliefs were partially responsible for their failure. Night, for the Inca, was sacred to the gods. Their religion prevented night attacks, except at special times. This meant losing a real advantage, especially at the new moon, when they had to spend the darkest night offering sacrifices and drinking chicha. Fighting was permitted only once in twenty nights, during the full moon, when they were easy targets for harquebusiers and crossbowmen.

Freedom from night attacks allowed the Spaniards to rest easily and make needed repairs. Ruined buildings were pulled down to give the cavalry room to maneuver, and defenses were strengthened. Spaniards mended the roofs of their quarters, replacing flammable thatch with wood covered by earth.

Cuzco had no wells; drinking water came only from two small rivers that flowed through the city. European sieges always began with the attackers cutting the water supply. Not the Inca. For some unknown reason, they failed to dam the rivers or divert them into other channels.

Hernando Pizarro, however, made full use of his resources. Rather than wait for Manco to attack, he carried out an aggressive defense. Often squadrons of cavalry set out on what we would call "search and destroy" missions. These missions had a twofold objective. First, they took prisoners to be tortured for information. They also sought to kill as many Indians as possible.

Search and destroy missions were dangerous, as Pedro Pizarro discovered. During a skirmish, Pedro, not noticing that he'd become separated from his companions, kept on lancing Incas. But when he wished to turn back, his horse stepped into a hole and fell, throwing him to the ground. Seeing their chance, the Indians rushed up and, while one led Pedro's horse away, the others pummeled Pedro with stones and maces. Luckily for him, his comrades realized that he was missing and returned at a gallop. They dashed through the Inca, shouting for Pedro to get between them and grab their stirrups. Then, shielding him with their horses, they ran with him to safety. He was bruised and breathless, but still very much alive.

During one of these search-and-destroy missions, the headless bodies of five Spanish messengers who had come from Lima at various times were found at a roadside. Fortunately, the Inca hadn't destroyed the messengers' mail pouches. These contained the first news of the outside world to reach Cuzco in months.

The Marquis knew about the siege and had sent relief parties three times. The Inca would allow them to enter a narrow gorge, block the entrances and exits, and then bury them under tons of rocks. None survived. The relief parties were wiped out, including a seventy-man cavalry unit—nearly as many horsemen as defended Cuzco.

Lima itself had been attacked in August 1536 by Quizo Yupanqui, Manco's best general. For two weeks Quizo stood outside Lima with a vast army. But Lima lies in flat, open country

Breaking the siege of Lima. In this drawing a Spaniard drives his lance into the Inca general in command of the besieging army.

ideal for cavalry actions. As the enemy advanced, a squadron of cavalry went straight for its center. Quizo was toppled from his litter and hacked to pieces, together with forty orejones. His army became a leaderless mob and scattered.

Help from outside enabled the Marquis to keep his foothold on the coast. Ever since his brother Hernando had brought home to Spain the "royal fifth" of the Inca loot, gold-rush fever had swept the Spanish Empire. On some Caribbean islands, there was danger of whole colonies disappearing as settlers flocked to Peru. The governor of Puerto Rico, for instance, tried everything to prevent settlers from leaving. He pleaded with them to remember their duty as Spaniards. When words failed he took harsher measures. "Some were whipped," he wrote, "and others had their feet cut off." Yet Spaniards continued to go to Peru in growing numbers.

When the rebellion began, the Marquis had sent appeals for aid throughout Spanish America. His appeals were answered and, by the time Quizo Yupanqui appeared outside Lima, help was arriving. From Nicaragua came a large warship with supplies and horses. The governors of Guatemala and Honduras sent fighting men. Scores of Hernán Cortés's veterans set out from Mexico. A hundred cavalry and two hundred infantry arrived from Panama. King Charles even sent a hundred of his own harquebusiers and crossbowmen.

The Spanish buildup continued as the native effort slackened. By late August 1536, Inca food supplies were low, forcing Manco into a double bind. To avoid mass starvation, he had to send most of his warriors back to their fields, making it easier for the Spaniards to relieve Cuzco and conquer the Inca permanently. Or he could continue the siege in the hope of destroying the Spaniards, but with the certainty of famine. He chose to feed his people.

Every day thousands of Inca left their positions around Cuzco and headed home. A smaller force, though still numbering many thousands, continued the siege. But their efforts were halfhearted, and they had no chance of winning.

Hernando Pizarro sensed immediately that the balance had tipped in his favor. Since he was also short of food, he sent raiding parties to scour the countryside. Thousands of llamas were rounded up and driven to Cuzco; maize was taken from hungry natives. Wherever the Spaniards passed, they left behind a desert of burned villages and fields.

The struggle became evermore ruthless. "I can bear witness," wrote conquistador Alonzo Enríquez de Guzman, "that this was the most dreadful and cruel war in the world. For between Christians and [Muslims] there is some fellow-feeling, and it is in the interests of both sides to spare those they take alive because of their ransoms. But in this Indian war there is no such feeling on either side. They give each other the cruellest deaths they can imagine."

The Inca tortured Spanish prisoners to death. The Spaniards answered in kind. Gonzalo Pizarro, for example, captured two hundred natives during a raid. But instead of killing them, he cut off their right hands and sent them back as a warning to the rest. Others were burned alive or impaled on wooden posts. Hernando Pizarro ordered his men to torture and kill women captives in full view of their menfolk. The shrieks of the women resounded across the valley, tormenting the most hardened warriors, who could do nothing to save them. Hernando's idea was to spread terror while depriving the warriors of those who did the camp chores. "The strategem worked admirably and caused much terror," a Spaniard boasted. "The Indians feared to lose their wives, and the latter feared to die." Such calculated cruelty showed the Inca that they'd met their equals in terrorism.

And so it went until April 1537, when Diego de Almagro returned from Chile. Upon Almagro's arrival, Manco's armies melted away, taking with them the last hope of Inca liberty. The Sapa Inca led a few hundred supporters into the mountainous Vilcabamba region north of Cuzco to wage a long, fruitless, guerrilla war.

At least 20,000 Inca died in the siege of Cuzco. Spanish losses were about 350, of whom about 300 were settlers killed in the countryside or in the ambush of relief columns. Hernando Pizarro lost very few men, a remarkable achievement given the odds he faced.

Still the tragedy of the Conquest continued. Victorious against the Inca, the Spaniards now turned their weapons against one another.

5

HONOR
AMONG THIEVES

DIEGO DE ALMAGRO HAD LEFT FOR CHILE IN JULY
1535 with a well-equipped force of 570 Spaniards and thousands
of Indian porters. They got off to a good start. Spirits were high,
for soon they expected to be rolling in gold.

Week after week, they moved along the Inca road that followed the high plain to the south. Nearing Chile, however, the
road ended and they began to wander among trackless mountains.
It was like the march to Cajamarca, only worse. Wherever they
turned, they faced canyons and passes with dizzying heights and
sheer drops. The altitude drained their energy, making each step
more difficult. Blue-green pine forests seemed to go on forever,
deep and dark.

The cold became unbearable as windblasts swept down from
frozen mountaintops. Frostbite claimed fingers, toes, and sometimes entire limbs. Men, blinded by the gleaming snow, depended
on comrades to lead them. Anyone too exhausted to go on
dropped by the wayside and fell asleep in the cold—a sleep from
which he never awoke.

The natives, miserable in open sandals and thin cottons, died in droves. Food was so scarce, and the Spaniards so unfeeling, that the survivors had to feed on their comrades' bodies, until their turn came to fall. Rather than feed them, it was easier for the Spaniards to replace the porters with other unfortunates. Whenever they came to a village, men, women, and children were kidnapped. Like beasts of burden, they were then chained together by the neck in groups of ten to twelve.

Almagro used the Indians as needed, not caring how he used them up. By day, they carried heavy loads uphill for hours without rest. The Spaniards' animals were more precious to them than

Indian porters died by the thousands during Diego de Almagro's expedition to Chile. Almagro cared nothing for the Indians' welfare and made them carry heavy loads and march nearly naked in the high Andes.

Indian lives. When some mares gave birth, Indian women were made to carry the foals in litters. Soldiers also had themselves carried in litters, leading their horses by the halters so as not to tire them. By night, the Indians were kept in open holding pens, where many froze. Father Cristóbal de Molina tells us: "When one Indian died they cut off his head to terrify the others and to avoid undoing their shackles or opening the padlock on the chain."

Soldiers prided themselevs on their cruelty. Anyone who killed many natives became a celebrity in camp. Anyone who showed mercy to them or stood up for them was considered a weakling. As a result, the natives came to hate Almagro. His patrols were ambushed and soldiers mutilated. In reprisal for one ambush, he had thirty chiefs burned alive. Though he was hard and cruel, he was good to his soldiers. They loved him and would follow him anywhere.

Almagro discovered there were no cities to capture in Chile, no coricanchas to loot. The farther the force advanced, the greater their disappointment, and the more Almagro brooded about his claim to Cuzco. When he turned back after marching a thousand miles, he had convinced himself that Cuzco belonged to his province of New Toledo. Not all the Pizarros on earth would keep him from his capital.

Almagro first learned of Manco's rebellion on the road back to Cuzco. Despite the long siege, Cuzco was still in Spanish hands. As his army neared the city, the remaining Inca were driven away, and Almagro prepared to claim his prize. He meant to claim it peacefully if possible, forcibly if necessary.

He sent a messenger to Hernando Pizarro to demand that Cuzco be turned over to him immediately. Hernando was outraged. He despised Almagro; insulting him was a favorite pastime. And now Almagro demanded Cuzco, after the Pizarros had shed their blood for it. Never! After some more choice words, the messenger was sent back to Almagro's camp.

Toward midnight of April 8, 1537, the Men of Chile, as Almagro's followers called themselves, marched into Cuzco. Moving swiftly, they blocked the roads with squadrons of cavalry and seized key buildings on Joy Square. Rodrigo de Orgóñez, Almagro's second-in-command, led the assault on the Pizarros' quarters. The building was guarded by twenty soldiers, and there was plenty of swordplay around the doors until Orgóñez had the roof set on fire. Soon burning rafters were falling on the defenders' heads, forcing them to surrender. Just as they stepped outside, the roof collapsed with a roar.

In the days that followed, the Men of Chile took whatever they wanted from the Pizarros' followers. The brothers Hernando and Gonzalo Pizarro were thrown into a dungeon until Almagro decided what to do with them.

Orgóñez urged him to cut their heads off immediately. *"El muerto no morde"*—"The dead do not bite"—he said, quoting a Spanish proverb. Better to have done with the Pizarros right away than to go on worrying about them. Almagro had wounded their pride. They might smile and say all is forgiven, but those were meaningless gestures. The Pizarros never forgot an injury. They'd bide their time, then take revenge. Almagro ignored the advice. He locked the Pizarros up and went to deal with one of the Marquis's captains who'd come too close for comfort.

Francisco Pizarro had sent yet another force to break the Inca siege of Cuzco. That force, led by Alonso de Alvarado, a veteran Indian fighter from Guatemala, was now forty miles west of Cuzco. When he learned of its presence, Almagro sent ambassadors to demand its surrender. But the moment his ambassadors arrived, Alvarado put them in chains and advised the Marquis what had happened. There was no choice now: If Almagro wanted to keep Cuzco, he'd have to fight.

Almagro found Alvarado's troops camped across the Abancay River, a small, swift stream that flows into the Apurímac. The main force guarded a bridge, while a large detachment was posted at a ford downstream. It was a strong position, but not strong enough, because there was a traitor in Alvarado's camp.

One of Alvarado's officers bore him a grudge and chose this

time to pay him back. He secretly wrote to Almagro, advising him to mass his troops opposite the bridge in daylight but to send a cavalry squadron across the ford at night. If Almagro did that, he, the traitor, would do his part. Almagro agreed and made his preparations for the assault.

On the evening of July 12, 1537, Orgóñez led his cavalry to the riverbank. No effort was made to conceal their presence. Whooping and cheering, they splashed across the ford and up the embankment on the other side. During the confusion, the traitor, stationed nearby, allowed Orgóñez to gain a foothold. Meantime, Alvarado, hearing sounds of battle, rushed to the ford with the bulk of his troops, leaving the bridge lightly guarded. That's when Almagro struck. He swept across the bridge and attacked Alvarado from behind, forcing him to surrender. Once again the Men of Chile had humiliated the Marquis.

At this point, Almagro became drunk on his own success. He'd won twice and saw no reason why he shouldn't do so again. After putting things in order in Cuzco, he started for the coast, determined to make the Marquis recognize his claims or to destroy him in battle. Gonzalo Pizarro and Alonso de Alvarado were left behind under heavy guard; Hernando Pizarro was taken along as a hostage.

Francisco Pizarro knew more than one way to defeat an opponent. Instead of offering battle, he offered words. In November 1537, he invited Almagro to discuss their differences. Gonzalo had escaped by then and reached Lima, which strengthened Francisco's bargaining power enormously.

Now, to gain Hernando's freedom, Francisco promised that Almagro could keep Cuzco until the king decided its owner once and for all. Almagro agreed and the two men embraced, vowing never again to quarrel. To show that there were no hard feelings, Hernando was sent back to Cuzco with a guard of honor. The guard was commanded by an eighteen-year-old known as El Joven, "the Lad," Almagro's son Diego by an Indian woman of Panama.

Almagro's officers, however, were not pleased with the agreement. They knew that the Marquis would say anything to have his way, but that his words were worthless. When Orgóñez heard its terms, he took his beard in one hand and passed the other across his throat in a cutting motion. "What has my loyalty to my commander cost me!" he moaned. It had cost him plenty. Before long it would cost him everything.

The Marquis had never meant to keep his part of the bargain. Within hours of Hernando's release, Francisco held a council of war. The agreement, he said, had been forced upon him and was therefore illegal. Almagro was a traitor and must be punished. Since the Marquis was too old to command in battle, Hernando would lead the army, seconded by Gonzalo.

Almagro was stunned when he heard of the betrayal. Yet he shouldn't have been, for Francisco Pizarro had been double-crossing him for years. A gullible man, Almagro had learned nothing from those experiences. And now he'd pay the price of ignorance. By trusting Pizarro one more time, he'd doomed not only himself, but those around him.

Almagro's self-confidence slipped away. He became confused, unable to act boldly. Although Orgóñez advised him to fight immediately, Almagro withdrew to Cuzco. That gave the Pizarros time to build up their forces. Then he failed to guard the mountain passes.

The showdown came on April 25, 1538, at Las Salinas, the "Saltpits," southeast of Cuzco. It was a marvelous day for the Indians. The Spaniards, for a change, were about to slaughter one another instead of them. As the armies took their positions, thousands of Indians crowded the hillsides, eager for the spectacle.

Almagro, like the Marquis, could no longer fight in person. Feeble, his body rotted by disease, he handed over command to Orgóñez. The Men of Chile numbered about five hundred and were strongest in artillery. The Pizarros had the advantage in everything else. Their seven hundred men were divided evenly between cavalry and foot soldiers. The harquebusiers, recently arrived from Europe, carried an improved weapon. Their guns used chain shot: two heavy balls connected by a length of chain. When fired, the balls spun through the air like a buzz saw, causing ghastly wounds.

Gonzalo began the assault at the head of the infantry. As they advanced, Orgóñez's cannon tore gaps in their ranks. Men toppled over, screaming; others disintegrated, pieces of them flying in different directions. But Gonzalo wouldn't let them retreat. He ran among the ranks, shouting and swinging with the flat of his sword to drive them forward. They rallied and, coming within range, blazed away with chain shot. Orgóñez's gunners fell alongside their weapons.

Hernando led the cavalry in a headlong charge across the field. *"El Rey y Pizarro!"* "The King and Pizarro!" they shouted, urging one another onward. *"El Rey y Almagro!"* "The King and Almagro!" Orgóñez's men answered as they galloped toward them. The two forces met with a crash that echoed off the hillsides. Dozens of men and horses went down in a welter of blood and dust. The natives, waving colored cloths and blowing conchshell trumpets, cheered the battle on.

Orgóñez was in the thick of the fight. Three times he chose an opponent, charged, and ran him through with his lance. He'd turned to face a fourth man when chain shot grazed his helmet, knocking him to the ground; another chain shot killed his mount. Dazed, Orgóñez stood up as enemy horsemen circled around him. He would have fought any of them man to man, but these odds were hopeless. Orgóñez surrendered and handed his sword to the nearest horseman. As he did, the man stabbed him in the heart. The soldiers then cut off his head and stuck it on a spear for display as a trophy.

Orgóñez's death ended the Battle of Las Salinas. The Men of Chile ran away, the enemy in hot pursuit. Almagro, who'd been watching from a hilltop, fled to Cuzco on a gentle old mule. Left behind were one hundred fifty Spanish bodies.

The natives were overjoyed. While the Pizarros' troops were busy in Cuzco, they came down to rob the dead. They worked quickly, efficiently, taking everything. At last the plain was quiet, except for the gabble of vultures roaming among naked corpses.

Although several of Almagro's captains were killed when captured, their leader was saved for special treatment. Before the battle, when told that Almagro might die of natural causes, Hernando exclaimed, "Heaven forbid that this should come to pass before he falls into my hands!" This tells a lot about Hernando's character. Not only did he want revenge, but it had to be "enjoyable." He must humiliate his victim, see him squirm before he found release in death.

Hernando played his own private game with Almagro. To cheer him up, he visited him in prison. Hernando was all smiles and sweet talk, promising that Almagro would be released when the Marquis arrived, although somehow the Marquis was always being delayed. Hardly a day passed without Hernando sending Almagro food from his own table to strengthen him. Almagro recovered and began to take a new lease on life.

Meantime, Hernando had invited anyone who'd been wronged by the prisoner to testify against him in secret. Suddenly it was as if Diego de Almagro was the devil himself. Enemies sprang up everywhere, each with a grievance. Men who'd benefited from his generosity now denounced him as a criminal. The testimony accumulated from week to week, until it filled two thousand closely written pages.

Almagro was charged with rebellion and treason and tried for his life. It was another mock trial, murder disguised as law. The accused was not present at the trial, and he had no opportunity to answer the charges. His judges were Hernando Pizarro and some officers whose names were not recorded. But their sentence was beheading.

When a priest informed Almagro of the sentence, he couldn't believe his ears. He'd always been a loyal subject of King Charles.

Three scenes in one picture. Diego de Almagro is arrested in the foreground, strangled at the right, and beheaded on the left. Sixteenth-century artists often used this technique to show action in different stages.

By seizing Cuzco, he'd only taken back what others had taken from him. The priest repeated the sentence and left the cell. Now, perhaps, Almagro understood how Atahuallpa had felt after *his* mock trial. Almagro had been one of the judges then, and that injustice had returned to haunt him.

Recovering his composure, Almagro asked to see Hernando Pizarro. The Marquis's brother came gladly, eagerly, to gloat over his enemy's misery. Almagro pleaded that he and the Marquis had been partners for years; Peru never would have been discovered without his aid. He warned that he was governor of New Toledo, and anyone who harmed him would have to answer to King Charles. Finally, in desperation, he reminded Hernando that he'd spared his life when he'd held him captive in that very same cell.

Not a flicker of sympathy crossed Hernando's eyes. He taunted Almagro as a coward, pointing out that it was shameful that an old soldier should beg for his life. "Make your peace with God," Hernando sneered, turning to leave, "and prepare yourself for death."

That night (July 8, 1538), as Diego de Almagro slept, two men entered his cell. One, a priest, said Almagro had been granted the favor of dying in private. The other, an executioner, then strangled him as Atahuallpa had been strangled. Almagro's body was taken to Joy Square, where his head was cut off with a single blow of an ax.

With Almagro's death, Peru settled down to an uneasy peace. The Marquis rewarded his followers with vast estates and the Indians to work on them. His brothers benefited most. Hernando had thousands of acres of land and the governorship of Cuzco. Gonzalo ruled Quito and received land along the present Peru-Bolivia border. The Marquis busied himself with building his capital, governing, and raising a family. He lived like a prince in a palace on Lima's main square, opposite the cathedral. Although he never married, he lived with one of Atahuallpa's half sisters. Doña Inéz, as the Spaniards called her, was fifteen when she bore Pizarro a daughter, Francisca, toward the end of 1534. He was delighted with the child and often played with her—the only tender moments that have been recorded from his life. A son, Gonzalo, died in childhood.

Yet there was no peace between the Marquis and the Sapa Inca, Manco. Unable to match his enemy in open battle, Manco learned the art of guerrilla warfare. From hideouts in Vilcabamba, he raided plantations, drove off cattle, and killed settlers. Groups of travelers were attacked and killed outright or made to linger under torture. Wherever he went, Manco encouraged the Indians to rebel. Those who aided the Spaniards were killed; he even tried to starve out the invaders by destroying the Indians' own crops.

INCA AND SPANIARD

Detachments sent after him were ambushed in mountain passes; one thirty-man party was annihilated and their heads stuck on poles.

If the search parties sent to find him were too strong, Manco escaped along secret trails and hid in the mountains. One of his hideouts was probably the "lost city" of Machu Picchu, "Old Peak," a sprawling complex of fortresses, palaces, and temples. Perched high above the gorge of the Urubamba River, only fifty miles northeast of Cuzco, Machu Picchu was abandoned sometime after the Conquest. The Spaniards never learned of it, and it remained unknown to outsiders until it was rediscovered by the American scientist Hiram Bingham in 1912.

The "lost city" of Machu Picchu was found by the American explorer Hiram Bingham in 1912. It is believed that the rebel Inca Manco used it as a hideout after the failure of his rebellion.

Toward the end of 1539, the Marquis sent Gonzalo to hunt down the rebels. Spaniards, led by Cañari scouts, attacked Manco's camp one night after everyone had gone to sleep. The Sapa Inca himself escaped at the last moment, but some of his people were captured. Among them was his favorite sister-wife, the same Cura Ocllo who'd been abused by Gonzalo before the rebellion.

Once again, the Marquis decided to offer words instead of battle. An African slave was sent to Vilcabamba with a gift for Manco and an invitation to discuss their differences. The Sapa Inca did not receive the envoy graciously; indeed, he had the slave killed, along with the gift, a fine horse.

The Marquis, boiling with rage, took out his anger on a helpless woman. He had Cura Ocllo stripped naked and paraded before the Spanish army. She was then tied to a tree and whipped by Cañari warriors. Yet she wouldn't give Pizarro the satisfaction of crying out or begging for mercy. The soldiers were amazed that a woman could show such courage. Pedro Pizarro tells us: "The Spaniards who were present there said that this Indian woman never spoke a word or uttered a complaint. . . . It is a thing worthy of admiration that a woman should neither complain nor speak nor make any moaning even in the pain of her wounds in the moment of death." After the Cañari shot her with arrows, her body was put into a basket and floated down a river for Manco to find.

This brutal murder encouraged more guerrilla attacks, which in turn encouraged more Spanish atrocities. In their lust for vengeance, each side took an eye for an eye and a tooth for a tooth, until it seemed that everyone would be blind and toothless. To deal with the attacks, the Marquis built settlements in key areas. Trujillo, Callao, Arequipa, and San Miguel de la Piura were built on the coast to keep open seaborne communications; Ayacucho guarded the road between Lima and Cuzco. These settlements were military outposts, much like those the Inca had built in conquered territory. While Indians did the farmwork, settlers stood ready to spring to arms at the least sign of trouble.

The Indians were not the only ones who hated Francisco Pizarro. He had never forgiven the Men of Chile for having turned against him. As punishment, he made their lives miserable. He took from Diego de Almagro, the Lad, all his father's property. The other Men of Chile lost their lands and money and were forced into poverty. Things were so bad that twelve ex-soldiers had to live in the same house. Since there was only one cloak among them, and since a Spanish gentleman wouldn't be seen in public without a cloak, only one man could leave the house at a time.

Driven to despair, the Men of Chile looked to the Lad as their natural leader. The Marquis had allowed the Lad not only to live in Lima, but to have a house across the square from his own palace. Often the Men of Chile gathered in his house at night. They'd reminisce about the old days, share their hatred of the Pizarros, and plan their revenge.

Word of these meetings reached the Marquis at the moment he lost his most trusted adviser. Late in 1539, Hernando Pizarro left for Spain with more gold for the king and to explain the death of the elder Almagro. Before sailing, he warned his brother about the Men of Chile. He begged Francisco to prevent them from gathering and to form a bodyguard for his own protection. But Francisco only laughed at such "idle fears." He was lord of New Castile and, for all he cared, his enemies could choke on their hatred. They wouldn't dare raise a finger against him.

Hernando reached Spain late in 1540. King Charles welcomed the gold he brought, but not its bearer. He'd known about Almagro's mock trial for months and he wasn't pleased. Although Hernando was never charged with a crime, the king had him arrested and jailed.

He was not put in an ordinary jail, but one suitable to his rank and contributions to Spain. For twenty years Hernando lived in a castle where a king of France had once been held captive. Servants waited on him hand and foot. He ate the best foods, wore the finest clothes, and slept in a bedroom hung with gorgeous tapestries. Visitors came and went freely, among them his niece, Francisca, the daughter of Francisco and Doña Inéz. Hernando and Francisca married in 1552, when she was eighteen and he fifty-four. She shared his confinement for the next eight years, giving birth to five children. Released in 1560, the couple retired to Trujillo in Extremadura. There Hernando lived for eighteen more years, a bitter old man clinging to his fortune. He outlived all his brothers and was the only one of them to die quietly in bed.

In the meantime, King Charles worried about New Castile. Its governor was an ambitious man, and the king didn't like ambitious men operating so far from home. Being far away from royal power gave such men dangerous ideas about their own importance. Perhaps the Marquis had such ideas. Perhaps he saw Peru as an independent country with himself as King Francisco. King Charles had to know for sure if Pizarro was loyal.

In the autumn of 1540, he sent someone to see what was really happening in Peru. Judge Cristóbal Vaca de Castro, a trustworthy man of learning and common sense, was chosen for the mission. The judge had two sets of instructions. The first set, which was made public, ordered him to cooperate with the marquis in all matters. The second set was secret; in case of the marquis's death, the judge was to take over as governor. The king was wise to issue these instructions; for when Vaca de Castro arrived at Quito, he received startling news. Several weeks earlier, His Excellency Don Francisco Pizarro, Governor of New Castile, had been assassinated in Lima.

The assassins were led by Juan de Rada, an officer as loyal to the Lad as he'd been to his father. Rada's plan was to kill the Marquis on Sunday, June 26, 1541. The Marquis always attended Sunday mass at Lima cathedral. After services, as he walked home, twenty Men of Chile would burst from the Lad's house and

161

stab the Marquis to death in the street. In the confusion that followed, Pizarro supporters would be arrested and the Lad made governor.

One of the plotters, however, had second thoughts. Troubled by his conscience, he confessed the plot to a priest, who promptly told the Marquis. But Pizarro was so arrogant, so sure that nothing could happen to him, that he dismissed the warning. The priest, he said, smiling smugly, had made up the story to get a reward. After much debate among his advisers, it was decided that he'd miss church just this one time. He took no other precautions, nor did he investigate the priest's claim.

On that fatal Sunday, Rada and his accomplices met in the Lad's house. They waited impatiently, peering through cracks in the door to catch sight of their victim. Minutes passed, then hours, without the Marquis showing himself. Puzzled, they looked at each other, wondering what had gone wrong. The mystery was solved when a comrade brought word that Pizarro was "ill" and wouldn't be attending church that day. That news sent a bolt of fear through the would-be assassins. Their plot may have been discovered! At that moment Pizarro might be giving orders for their arrest! They had to act immediately or lose everything!

Soon the door of the Lad's house flew open and twenty men poured into the square. "Long live the king! Death to the tyrant!" they shouted, running toward the palace with drawn swords. As they crossed the square, one man turned aside to avoid a puddle. Rada sent him away with a curse. "We go to bathe in human blood," he snapped, "and you refuse to put your feet into a puddle of water!"

Their cries, so unusual for a Sabbath afternoon, attracted onlookers. "Who is the tyrant?" someone asked a friend. "Oh, the Marquis, I suppose. They are going to kill him," the friend answered coolly. Yet none would lift a finger to save him. Francisco Pizarro was rich and powerful and feared, but he wasn't loved, even by the people of his capital.

162

The assassins reached the palace gate and, finding it open, went inside. A servant who stood in their way was cut down, while another, fleeing only steps ahead of them, gave the alarm. Pizarro was dining upstairs with some officials who'd come to visit him during his "illness." But no sooner did they hear the servant's shout, than they leaped from the windows to the garden below. The Marquis, to whom they'd pledged eternal loyalty, was left with his half brother, Martin de Alcantara, an officer named Chaves, and two servants.

The assassins were running down a narrow passageway to the dining room when the Marquis told Chaves to bar the door. Had

Théodore de Bry's interpretation of Pizarro's assassination. As Almagro the Lad's men burst through the door, Pizarro's guests leap from the window. Although they owed Pizarro their jobs and wealth, none loved him enough to risk their lives on his behalf.

he done so, the two brothers would have had time to buckle on their corselets, armor covering the body from neck to waist. Chaves, however, had another idea, and it killed them all. Instead of barring the door, he held it ajar while he tried to reason with the assassins. They were not about to listen to reason. One of them reached in, stabbed Chaves in the heart, and kicked his body aside.

As they burst into the room, Martin de Alcantara, who'd been helping Francisco with his armor, ran to the doorway with the two servants. A furious battle followed. Swords glinted in the candle-light, then, striking home, turned red. Two Men of Chile, then the two servants, fell to the floor and lay in the center of widening pools of blood. Martin de Alcantara, wounded time and again, was felled by a thrust to the chest.

With that, Pizarro, unable to adjust his corselet alone, threw it away. Danger stirred his soldier's heart. Wrapping his left arm with a cloak, he drew his sword for the last time. "What ho!" he roared. "Traitors! Have you come to kill me in my own house?"

Steel clanged against steel as he went for them. He was still a good man with a sword, and he made the assassins pay for their boldness. He parried a thrust, lunged, and an assailant fell at his feet. Another died screaming. His companions drew back—but just for a moment.

When Rada saw this, he became angry. "Why are we so long about it? Down with the tyrant!" he cried. As he did so, he grabbed a man and deliberately pushed him onto Pizarro's blade. The blade went in halfway to the hilt, and before Pizarro could with-draw it, a sword pierced his throat. Reeling, blood spurting from his mouth, he fell to the floor. "Jesu," he gasped, tracing a cross on the floor with his own blood. As he bent over to kiss the sacred sign, the assassins ran him through.

He died, in the words of the historian Francisco López de Gómara, "with none even to say, God forgive him." Yet who can say that this was not the death he preferred? Seventy years old, he'd always lived by the sword, and now he'd died by it. And he'd died fighting, like a son of Extremadura.

164

The Men of Chile take their revenge. Francisco de Pizarro had lived by the sword and, at last, died by it.

The Men of Chile rushed into the square, happy at their revenge. "The tyrant is dead!" they shouted through the streets of Lima. "The laws are restored! Long live our master the emperor, and his governor, Almagro!" To celebrate their triumph, they looted Pizarro's palace and the houses of his followers. Pizarro's body, hastily buried within hours of his death, rests today in a tomb near the main door of Lima cathedral.

Every Spanish town was forced to recognize the Lad as governor. Anyone who refused, and many did, lost their jobs and property. Vincente de Valverde, Bishop of Cuzco, was among the losers. He was allowed to leave Peru, but his ship ran aground on Puna Island, where the Indians, remembering Pizarro's visit, massacred everyone. It was said that the Indians slowly cut Valverde to pieces with sharpened clam shells. Although the Punans hated the Inca, without knowing it they'd avenged Atahuallpa.

Pizarro's assassins didn't enjoy themselves for long. In killing him, they not only made enemies of his followers, but declared war on their king. Whatever King Charles thought of Pizarro, he was

165

still a royal governor. A blow against him was the same as a blow against royalty and not to be tolerated.

When Vaca de Castro heard of the assassination, he showed his secret instructions. As governor, he declared that every citizen must help him punish Pizarro's murderers or be branded a traitor. Treason was the one crime for which there could be no pardon. It was a crime not only against the king, but against God Almighty, by whose authority kings were said to rule. Spaniards punished violators of the "divine right of kings" with "drawing and quartering." The traitor was taken to the place of execution in a cage. As everyone watched, the executioner slit open his belly, tore out his intestines, and threw them in his face while he was still alive. He was then beheaded and his body hacked into quarters, which were displayed on hooks at the town gates. There they stayed until they rotted away, gruesome reminders of the fate awaiting traitors.

The Pizarros' followers were not the only ones to join the new governor. There were Spaniards everywhere who believed the Men of Chile had gone too far. During the next year, volunteers flocked to Vaca de Castro's banner until he was ready to bring the traitors to justice. His march southward was less a military expedition than a triumphal procession, as one town after another opened its gates to him; finally Lima declared its loyalty. All that remained was to retake Cuzco.

On September 16, 1542, the two armies met on the plain of Chupas near Ayacucho. Although the loyalists outnumbered the Men of Chile seven hundred to five hundred, the Men of Chile had the advantage. They held the crest of a gently rising hill. Their cavalry were massed to the right and left, with sixteen cannon clustered between them. It was a strong position and they meant to hold it at all costs.

There were the usual cavalry charges, but the heroes of the day were the loyalist infantry led by Francisco de Carvajal. If those who knew him were correct, he was seventy-five, having spent forty of those years on the battlefields of Europe. Standing

166

over six feet tall, he weighed two hundred fifty pounds and swung a battle-ax as easily as feather. He had a deep, booming voice and swore like a demon.

Carvajal led his men straight for the cannon. Tongues of orange flame leaped from the iron muzzles, followed by clouds of white smoke. Cannonballs plowed the hillside, tearing great holes in the oncoming ranks. The infantry wavered; some even began a panicky retreat. But their commander was not one to tremble at the sight of blood and bodies. He threw off his armor and ran to the front, waving his sword over his head. "Shame on you, my men!" he roared. "Do you give way now! I am twice as good a mark for the enemy as any of you!" The soldiers rallied, took the cannon, and swept on to victory.

Vaca de Castro was merciless toward traitors. After the battle, he searched among the prisoners for those involved in the Marquis's murder or in the Lad's seizure of power. Thirty were found and quartered. Those who'd joined the Lad only after he'd occupied Cuzco were shown leniency; they were set free, after losing their right hands. Never again would they draw a sword against their king. The Lad himself was spared a traitor's death in consideration of his father's services to the crown. He was taken to Cuzco and beheaded on the same spot where his father's body had been displayed.

The rebellion crushed, Vaca de Castro gave Peru firm, honest government until the next explosion.

That explosion resulted from Spain's guilty conscience about the Indians. Abuse of the natives was nothing new when Pizarro landed in Peru. It began practically the moment Columbus arrived in the New World. As soon as he set eyes on the natives, a gentle people called the Tainos, Columbus wanted to enslave them. When he returned from his first two voyages, he took with him native people, several of whom were given to friends as gifts. Queen Isabella, however, had other ideas. She scolded her Admiral of the Ocean Sea for making slaves of the Indians and ordered them returned to their homeland immediately, at their owners' expense.

The New World, unfortunately, was far from Spain, and settlers could do pretty much as they pleased. Colonial governors usually turned a blind eye to the settlers' atrocities. Indians were enslaved, tortured, and worked to death. Bored settlers amused themselves by hunting them with crossbows. Natives of the Caribbean Islands—Hispaniola, Cuba, Puerto Rico—were all but exterminated within thirty years of the islands' discovery. The resulting labor shortage spurred the search for slaves elsewhere, which led to Cortés's discovery and conquest of Mexico.

Yet if Spain produced fierce conquistadores, it is to her glory that she also produced men of decency and conscience. As early as 1511, Friar Antonio de Montesinos, a Dominican, preached a sermon in a tiny church on Hispaniola. Settlers, he said, had no right to own Indians, let alone kill them for sport. Anyone who did so was in a state of "mortal sin" and would burn in hell. It wasn't a sermon people wanted to hear, and they dismissed Montesinos as a tenderhearted fool.

They could not dismiss Bartholomé de las Casas so easily. Las Casas had come to Hispaniola in 1498 at the age of twenty-four. Like his companions, he'd come seeking his fortune. But unlike them, he was sickened at what he saw. Those sights caused him to give up his land and become a Dominican friar, the first priest to be ordained in the New World. During the years that followed, he visited Cuba, Mexico, Guatemala, and Nicaragua. It was always the same: Wherever he went, he witnessed shocking cruelties toward the native people.

Las Casas used his pen as easily as conquistadores used their swords. He stabbed the Spanish conscience with books about what he'd seen. People respected him and, in time, he earned the title Protector of the Indians.

His most famous work was *The Very Brief Relation of the*

Bartholomé de las Casas was known as the Protector of the Indians and the father of the New Laws of the Indies. Spanish settlers hated the outspoken priest and, it is said, named their dogs after him.

Destruction of the Indies. This book is filled with examples of man's inhumanity to man. Such inhumanity was a scandal, a sin, deserving of divine punishment. "Should God decide to destroy Spain," Las Casas wrote, "this history will make it clear that Spain deserved the punishment for the destruction we have brought to the Indies."

The Very Brief Relation of the Destruction of the Indies is also an affirmation of human rights and religious faith. Las Casas argued that the Indians were free men equal to any, even Spaniards, in the eyes of God. Spaniards had no right to make war on them, torture them, take their women, enslave them. The Spaniards had, moreover, stained their country's honor in the name of religion. If the Indians worshipped false gods, it was due to igno-

169

rance, not wickedness. They must be taught the truth gently, lovingly. One could not teach Christianity with whips and swords.

Las Casas's words echoed in the hearts of many of his countrymen. Sometime in 1542, he gave King Charles the manuscript of his book. He couldn't have put it into better hands. True, the king wanted gold, but he also wanted a clean conscience. He would later give up the crown to spend his last years in a monastery to be closer to God.

Las Casas's work bore fruit in the New Laws of the Indies issued a few weeks after the battle of Chupas. In them the king declared that anyone who had Indian slaves could keep them during his lifetime, but, at his death, they had to be released. If, however, an owner mistreated his slaves, they were to be freed immediately. The king also ordered that no more Indians were to be enslaved and that free Indians must be paid fair wages for their work. Every slave owner and employer had to provide religious instruction at his own expense.

The New Laws landed like a bombshell in the colonies. Irate colonists bombarded Spain with petitions against the laws' "injustice." They'd conquered new lands for Spain and were entitled to enjoy the benefits, they said. Besides, they were so used to living by the labor of others they couldn't imagine any other way to survive. King Charles held firm: The New Laws must be obeyed.

Settlers in New Castile were especially upset. The New Laws contained a section dealing with them alone. Anyone who'd taken part in the Pizarro-Almagro feud automatically lost his lands and slaves. That meant *anyone,* regardless of whether he'd followed the governor or sided with the Men of Chile. In effect, nearly every conquistador suddenly became poor.

To guarantee that the New Laws were obeyed, the post of governor was abolished and replaced by the Royal Audience, a high court composed of four judges. Day-to-day government was in the hands of a viceroy, one who rules as the king's personal representative. The king chose Blasco Nuñez Vela to be the first viceroy of Peru.

Nuñez Vela was the worst choice for this important position. A stubborn man given to temper tantrums, he thought he could do no wrong. The judges who sailed with him believed him either stupid or insane. He may have been both.

Arriving in Panama, Nuñez Vela found a ship full of Peruvian silver that had been mined by slaves. The cargo was seized. Three hundred slaves were immediately freed on the viceroy's order, leaving settlers' crops to spoil in the fields. He even paid his Indian porters, a bad example, surely, in the eyes of slave owners. When settlers protested, he shouted that the law was the law, and he'd enforce it over their dead bodies if need be. Anyone who disagreed with him was threatened with a hundred lashes on the bare back, a terrible punishment that crippled even the strongest men.

By the time Nuñez Vela reached Lima in mid-1544, the settlers were determined to resist him. At the center of that resistance was Gonzalo Pizarro, the richest man in the country and the settlers' natural leader. He'd been dissatisfied with the way things had been going for years. At the time of his brother's murder, he'd been exploring the valley of the Amazon. He had returned in time to offer his services to Vaca de Castro, only to be turned down. It was a polite turndown, but it hurt his pride. His pride was hurt again by Nuñez Vela's appointment. As a Pizarro, Gonzalo claimed that he, not some court favorite, was best qualified to be viceroy. His family had conquered Peru and it seemed right that it should rule there forever.

Gonzalo was prepared to back his claim with force. He began to organize an army, under the excuse of fighting Manco's guerrillas. Old Carvajal helped him turn the army into the most powerful force in South America. When Nuñcz Vela ordered the army disbanded, Gonzalo refused and marched on the capital.

Meantime, Nuñez Vela was making one mistake after another. He began to distrust everyone, including his own officials. One day he accused an aide of disloyalty. When the man protested, Nuñez Vela drew a dagger and stabbed him to death. Although Nuñez Vela had the body buried secretly, it was soon discovered. The judges of the Royal Audience arrested Nuñez Vela and sent him back to Spain for trial on murder charges.

He had already left when Gonzalo arrived at the capital with his army. Lima's citizens went wild with joy. Welcoming him as their liberator, they declared Gonzalo governor and put the country in his hands completely. Those who disagreed either kept quiet or answered to Carvajal. He once arrested three of Lima's leading citizens and hung them outside the city. The idea of hanging "rebels" tickled his sense of humor. Two men were hung on the lower branches of a tree; the third, higher in rank, was allowed to choose the branch from which he'd hang. Carvajal then informed Lima's citizens that there were many sturdy trees outside their city. No wonder people called him the Demon of the Andes.

Nuñez Vela never reached Spain. He must have been good with words, for he convinced his guards to set him ashore at Tumbes. From there he went to Quito, where he announced that he was still viceroy and called for volunteers to fight the traitors. Several hundred men joined him, but they were no match for Gonzalo's force. On January 18, 1546, Nuñez Vela's force was defeated at Añaquito, a few miles north of Quito. Nuñez Vela's head was cut off and stuck on the point of a spear. The victors hated him so much that some plucked hairs from his beard and set them in their caps as souvenirs.

Gonzalo was now as powerful as his brother Francisco had ever been. More powerful. From Quito to Chile, Spaniards recognized Gonzalo's authority alone. Protected by a large bodyguard, he took on the trappings of royalty. He spoke of himself with the royal *we* instead of the commoner's *I*. When visitors came, he offered his hand to be kissed; no one, regardless of rank, was allowed to sit in his presence. Gonzalo, Spaniards whispered, was acting like a king. Indian servants saw him as a white Sapa Inca.

Carvajal advised him to go all the way by making himself king. "In fact," he said, "you have already done so. You have been in arms against a viceroy, have driven him from the country,

172

beaten and slain him in battle. What favor, or even mercy, can you expect from the Crown? You must go boldly on, proclaim yourself king; the troops, the people, will support you." He ended by begging him to marry an Inca princess and unite their two peoples as one family. Yet Gonzalo couldn't bring himself to take that final step.

Gonzalo met his match in Father Don Pedro de la Gasca, Nuñez Vela's replacement. A nobleman by birth, Gasca was already a successful soldier and lawyer at the age of thirty. But instead of following either of these careers, he studied for the priesthood and quickly became a bishop.

When Gasca heard that the king had chosen him to go to Peru, he said that he wanted nothing for himself. He asked for no salary or grand titles; he was satisfied to be president of the Royal Audience. What he wanted was power—unlimited power to do his job the right way. He wanted control over the government and courts of Peru. He wanted to be able to declare war, raise armies, and choose government officials. But most of all, he wanted authority to pardon any crimes and suspend any laws, including the New Laws.

The king's ministers gasped at Gasca's requests, for no Spanish subject had ever held such powers. King Charles, however, was willing to do anything to regain his richest colony. As proof of his trust, he gave Gasca everything he wanted—and more. King Charles sent Gasca a packet of papers that were blank except for the royal signature at the bottom of each sheet; Gasca could write anything he wanted above that signature. He would be, in effect, the king of Spain in the New World.

Gonzalo's supporters, the Pizarrists, breathed a sigh of relief when Gasca arrived in Panama. He was not an impressive figure. Small and thin, he wore the costume of a simple priest. He spoke calmly, softly, and was polite to everyone. During the weeks that followed, he met with Pizarrist leaders one by one. He told them that he meant them no harm, for he'd come on a mission of peace.

173

Bishop Don Pedro de la Gasca was sent to crush Gonzalo Pizarro's rebellion and bring order to Peru.

Their rebellion had succeeded. He had suspended the New Laws and would pardon everyone involved in the death of Nuñez Vela in return for their pledge of loyalty to the king. And, one by one, they joined him.

He even wrote to Gonzalo, offering to pardon him on the same terms. Gonzalo, however, wasn't interested in pardons. True, by submitting he'd save his life. But it wouldn't be a life worthy of a Pizarro. He'd be an ordinary citizen, a nobody in the land his family had conquered. There was only one thing to do: defend on the battlefield his right to rule. Gasca now had no choice but to raise an army and move south.

What followed was a confused series of moves and counter-moves as each side jockeyed for position. At first it seemed that Gonzalo would win. The Pizarrists were well armed and desper-

174

ate. They proved themselves by defeating one of Gasca's commanders at Huarina, southeast of Lake Titicaca, in October 1547. Yet that defeat was only a temporary setback. Gasca slowly rebuilt his forces with volunteers from Peru and from as far away as Mexico.

On April 9, 1548, the two armies met at the Cotapampa River outside Cuzco, almost at the exact spot where Huáscar had been defeated sixteen years earlier. But this time there was no pitched battle; indeed, there was no battle at all.

Gonzalo's men had no stomach for fighting King Charles's deputy in person. The two armies had taken their positions when a cavalry squadron, followed by a file of harquebusiers, broke ranks and joined Gasca's force. Once the desertions began, the scene became a stampede, with Gonzalo's men going over to the enemy by the hundreds. Without firing a shot or striking a blow, Gonzalo lost an empire.

He was stunned, unable to believe that his world was crumbling around him.

"What remains for us?" he asked one of the few captains who still stood by him.

"Fall on the enemy, since nothing else is left, and die like Romans," said the man.

Gonzalo shook his head. "Better to die like Christians," he replied in a half whisper. So saying, he rode toward the enemy lines to surrender.

Carvajal, seeing that all was lost, galloped away. He'd gone only a short distance when his horse stumbled, throwing him to the ground. Some of his own men, eager to win Gasca's pardon, captured him. So much for honor among thieves.

The Pizarrists paid the price of their treason. Ordinary soldiers were whipped until their backs resembled raw hamburger. Gonzalo was sentenced to be beheaded in Cuzco's main square. For years he'd robbed the Inca and now, like them, he was poor. Poorer than poor, for he owned absolutely nothing. All his possessions had been seized for the king; soon his mansion in Lima would be torn down and the lot strewn with salt so that nothing would grow where a traitor once stood. After a short speech in which he begged onlookers to pray for his soul, Gonzalo laid his head on a wooden block, and the executioner took it off with one stroke of his sword. The executioner then took Gonzalo's clothes as payment for his work. Carvajal was quartered and the body pieces strewn along the four roads leading out of Cuzco.

6

THE MASTERS OF NEW CASTILE

THE LAND OF THE FOUR QUARTERS WAS NO MORE. In its place stood New Castile, ruled by, and for, Spaniards. With the end of the civil wars, settlers began to arrive each year by the thousands. Sometimes they came alone, single men seeking their fortunes. Often, however, they brought wives and children, because New Castile was a good place to live—for Spaniards. It was different for the natives. The warlike Inca had lost everything in war: their families, their empire, their independence. Now they'd lose their way of life, becoming strangers in their own land.

The Spaniards gradually shaped the country to suit themselves. New towns sprang up, modeled on those they'd left behind. In the typical Spanish town, streets were laid out in a grid, long, straight, and crossing at right angles. At the town's center were the church, government buildings, and mansions of the wealthy grouped around a large square. The largest building was the church, for the Spaniards were a devout people and attended services regularly.

Inca cities were also remodeled along Spanish lines. The rebuilding of Cuzco began immediately after Manco's siege.

177

INCA AND SPANIARD

Sacsahuamán was dismantled and its ruins filled in with earth to prevent its use by rebels. The earthen mantle was removed in 1934, revealing portions of the walls scaled by Hernando Pizarro's men. Today, descendants of the Inca still drive llamas through narrow cobbled streets with Incan walls on either side. These walls, though, are the foundations of Spanish buildings, built with stones taken from Sacsahuamán. The coricancha survives, although in a different form. Much of the temple area was covered with earth and the Church of Santo Domingo built on top. When the church caved in during the 1950 earthquake, portions of the coricancha emerged, its walls intact after four centuries. Tourists visit the monks' cells, once chapels for the worship of Inca gods.

Yet, despite the rebuilding, sixteenth-century Cuzco stank like an open sewer. Its rivers, once so swift and pure, were polluted within fifteen years of Pizarro's entry. Mounds of garbage littered the riverbanks and the channels ran yellow with filth. Indians, who'd once bathed in the waters with their families, held their noses as they passed.

Cuzco was reserved for Spaniards. The Indians lived in slums on the outskirts, forbidden to enter without permission, and then only to work for their new masters. They were *los indios,* the "Indians," wretched creatures the Spaniards avoided whenever possible.

Some Indians, however, enjoyed special treatment. They were the beneficiaries of the Conquest. The Cañari were rewarded for their loyalty with land and privileges. They served as policemen, abusing their former masters with curses and clubs. Local chiefs continued to rule, so long as they did as they were told. Inca princesses married Spaniards, founding some of modern Peru's leading families. A few married noblemen, whose descendants are proud of their Inca heritage.

The conquistadores and settlers received land to encourage them to stay in New Castile. Once they took possession, they

178

began to import European animals and plants. Donkeys, pigs, cattle, and sheep were raised in large numbers. Wheat, grapes, and turnips grew easily in certain places.

Yet these didn't make up for the Spaniards' wastefulness and neglect. What the Inca had built over many generations, the Spaniards ruined within a few years. Roads were damaged by wheeled vehicles, which they weren't designed to handle. Irrigation canals and agricultural terraces were allowed to fall into disrepair. The storehouses, the people's insurance against crop failures, were looted and never restocked. Llamas were slaughtered for their brains, a delicacy among Spaniards, and the meat thrown away. Rather than shear the vicuña, they killed them for their wool. "The Spaniards did more harm in four years," an official wrote, "than the Incas had done in four hundred."

That was all right so far as most settlers were concerned. They hadn't come to the New World to work for a living. They'd come to live as gentlemen. A gentleman, a "son of someone," was a special person. He might be a soldier, marry into a wealthy family, or become a priest, but he never soiled his hands with work. Others worked for him.

In Spain, work was done by the common people for wages. But the common people of New Castile were native Indians, who knew nothing of money. In the past, when they worked, it had been for the state in return for a share of the produce. The necessities of life—food, clothing, tools—were stored by the government and distributed as needed. An Inca always knew how long he'd have to work and that he'd never be worked beyond his strength.

The Spaniards had come to take, not to give. To solve their labor problem, they forced the Indians to work. Whenever Spaniards set up a colony, they began a system called *encomienda*, meaning "to give in trust." A Spaniard received not only land, but the people to work on it. In Peru, no *encomendero*, "landowner," had fewer than five thousand Indian workers; some had forty thousand. These grants included entire villages, where every man, woman and child was bound to serve the master. In return, the master was supposed to protect them and help them become Christians.

An encomendero didn't live on his estate; indeed, he might only visit it on rare occasions. According to law, he had to live in a town, often hundreds of miles from his estate. Towns were strongholds, from which Spaniards could crush any rebellion that broke out. If they lived on their estates, rebels might kill them one at a time and destroy the country.

The produce of the encomendero's estate was brought to his town house several times a year. He lived very well. In the grants awarded by President de la Gasca, an encomendero was entitled to everything he, his family, and guests needed for a year. A typical encomendero received 2,500 pesos of gold and silver, 640 bushels of wheat, 800 bushels of barley, 200 bushels of maize, 30 llamas, 30 pigs, plus quantities of candles, tools, shoes, cloth, and rope—the list continues, filling a half page of small print.

The Indians who worked the encomendero's land were slaves in all but name. The New Laws were never brought back. In their place were other, less severe, laws intended to protect the Indians. They didn't; they were unenforced, remaining so much paper and ink. No viceroy would risk another settlers' rebellion for the Indians' sake.

In the writings of Felipe Guamán Pomo de Ayala we have an eyewitness account of what it was like for *los indios*. Guamán Pomo, "Hawk Puma," was an Indian who served the Spaniards as a minor official. He had to travel in the line of duty, and he saw a lot. Sometime after 1570, he described his experiences in a manuscript, *The New Chronicle and Good Government*, illustrated with hundreds of drawings. These are the best pictorial records we have of Inca life in early colonial times. It is a sad record—so sad, said Guamán Pomo, that "to write is to cry." Yet it is accurate and confirms what Spanish officials wrote about their fellow countrymen.

180

Guamán Pomo's indios were abused as few people in history have been. Indians were supposed to work hard, all day, every day, with little food and no rest. If one didn't produce his daily quota, he was clubbed and whipped; sometimes he was branded on the face with his master's initials. Indians were forced to grow their hair long, which served as a rope for dragging them around. When encomenderos visited their estates, they might amuse themselves by "dogging" their Indians; that is, hunting them with savage dogs for sport.

Spanish priests were often disliked by the Indians. Here, a crying woman, with a baby on her back, is abused by a Dominican friar while weaving a cloth for him.

181

Punishment was carried out by an overseer, one who supervised the farm work. Overseers were often black slaves from Africa. Spaniards depended on blacks to do much of their dirty work. Although slaves, the blacks were used in wartime to free whites for other duties, and they had a reputation for cruelty as great as the Spaniards themselves. Indians were terrified of them. One black, it was said, could keep a village in line with only a word and a whip.

"The law must be obeyed," says the caption of this picture. The law, of course, was Spanish law, and it had to be obeyed by the Indians, who were savagely punished for the slightest infractions.

The Indians were so downtrodden that some Spaniards pitied them. Hernando de Santillán, an official of the Royal Audience, reported about 1563:

They live the most wretched and miserable lives of any people on earth. As long as they are healthy they are fully occupied in working. . . . Even when they are sick, they have no respite, and few survive their first illness, however slight, because of the appalling existence they lead. They sleep on the ground . . . and their diet is maize, chili and vegetables; they never eat meat or anything of substance except some fish if they live on the coast. The only furnishings in their houses are some jars, pots, spindles, looms and other equipment for working. They sleep at night in the clothes they wear by day and scarcely succeed in clothing their children, most of whom are naked. . . . They are deeply depressed by their misery and servitude . . . and have come to believe that they must continue to work for the Spaniards for as long as they or their sons or descendants live, with nothing to enjoy themselves. Because of this they despair; for they ask only for their daily bread and cannot even have that. . . . There are no people on earth so hardworking, humble or well behaved.

Yet farm work was easy, compared to another type of labor. The Inca had always paid their taxes in the form of labor service for the community. The Spaniards kept the labor tax, especially for the mines. In 1545, silver was discovered at Potosí, in northern Bolivia, near the border of Peru. Potosí was not just a silver mine. It was a mountain laced with five thick veins of silver, the largest discovery of its kind ever made. Atahuallpa's ransom and the loot of Cuzco were tiny alongside the treasures of Potosí. For two centuries, it gave Spain hundreds of millions of dollars in precious metal. Potosí silver paid the king's armies, built his navy, and

CAPITVLODELOSPASAGEROS
ESPAÑOLESDELTA
bo ycriollos mestizos ymula
tos ycriollas mestizas yespa
ñoles cristianos
decastilla

Some Indians paid their labor tax by working as porters. If they displeased their masters, they were kicked and beaten, things no Spaniard would ever do to his horse.

financed his wars. Without it, Spain couldn't have become a mighty empire.

The weight of that empire rested on the backs of countless Indian miners. Each year thousands paid their labor tax at Potosí. They didn't pay willingly. When word came that the men of a certain village were drafted for the mines, panic swept the community. People knew that few would return as whole persons; returnees were usually crippled in body or mind from their ordeal. Most never returned.

184

The journey to the mines was itself a form of torture. Men left their villages amid moans and wails. Relatives chanted funeral dirges and pulled out their hair, because in their eyes the miners were already dead. They marched chained, with iron collars around their necks, for up to three months. Cold and hungry, they trudged from one mountain ridge to another. Brutal guards drove them to the limits of human endurance. One could easily follow their trail by the bodies strewn along the way.

Arriving at their destination, they found a city of 150,000, the largest in the New World. Potosí was a boom town of mining millionaires, gamblers, traders, and strong-arm men. King Charles had given it a coat of arms and a motto: "I am rich Potosí, treasure of the world and envy of kings." The Indians, however, didn't pause in the city, but were marched to their quarters at the mine. Actually, these quarters were prison camps where the miners were kept under armed guard and beaten for the slightest reason.

Entering the mine meant stepping into the world of the lost. A Spaniard told King Charles what it was like in 1550. "Some four years ago," he wrote, "there was discovered a mouth of hell into which a great mass of people enter every year and are sacrificed by the greed of the Spaniards to their 'god.' This is your silver mine called Potosí. . . . No one who knows the meaning of liberty can fail to see how this violates reason and the laws of freedom. . . . It is not the law of free men, which is how Your Highness describes these poor people in your provisions and ordinances." The king wanted the miners to be treated decently and paid fair wages. He meant well, but he also depended on silver too much to let anything slow production. And Indian lives were a small price to pay for Spain's world power. The labor tax was abolished only when Peru became independent in 1821.

A miner began his shift by climbing down rawhide ladders into the heart of the mountain 750 feet below. The ladders, rickety and worn, often broke, sending men hurtling to their deaths. Bodies were not removed; they were buried under slag heaps in abandoned tunnels.

Into the mouth of hell. Théodore de Bry shows Indians working in the silver mine of Potosí. In reality the mountain was not hollowed out; rather, the miners dug tunnels, following the five great veins of silver. Note that the men must work with a candle in one hand and a pick or hammer in the other.

Men worked naked, for it was hot so far underground, and they worked by candlelight. Each shift was divided into two teams. Diggers had to produce twenty-five one-hundred-pound sacks of ore each day or be whipped; Guamán Pomo's drawings show these unfortunates naked, hung upside down, their bodies covered with welts. Carriers lugged ore sacks up ladders on their backs, a climb lasting five hours. Each team worked five days and five nights at a stretch. Like moles, they ate underground, slept underground, and relieved themselves underground. Their sweaty bodies became crusted with dust and filth. Work was dangerous and there were always accidents. If, for example, a small pebble fell down the shaft, it hit with the force of a bullet. It was said that if twenty

186

healthy Indians went into the mine on Monday, ten would be dead or crippled by Saturday.

Potosí was linked to many other evils. Spaniards found an easy way to separate the silver from the ore in which it is found by using mercury. In this "mercury amalgamation process," the ore was crushed with hammers and mixed with mercury, a liquid metal also known as quicksilver. The mercury absorbed the silver in the ore; fire then vaporized the mercury, leaving nuggets of pure silver. Mercury mines were discovered near Potosí and thousands

Discipline at Potosí. Guamán Pomo shows Indians hung by the heels and whipped or, to make an example of them, tied to a llama naked and whipped through the camp. The man at the lower right has been let off "easy"; he must only spend a few days and nights with his feet locked in the stocks. If he survives the freezing nights, he'll be sent back to the mine.

of Indians were forced into them and made to work without safety precautions. The mine tunnels were filled with mercury dust, which workers inhaled. Mercury is a poison even in tiny doses, and nearly everyone caught *mal de mina*, "mine sickness," a painful disease ending in death.

Mine owners wanted to keep profits high and costs low. One way of doing this was to feed their Indians as little as possible, and work them as much as possible. The only problem was that the less people eat, the less work they can do. The owners solved the problem with coca. The tiny amount of cocaine found in coca leaves deadens feelings of hunger and fatigue. A worker may be starving and exhausted, yet, after chewing coca leaves, he will keep working until he drops dead.

The Inca rulers, we recall, knew about coca. They worshipped the plant, using it in religious ceremonies and as gifts for their nobility. It was so sacred, in fact, that commoners were forbidden to have it under any circumstances. This was a wise policy and prevented the people's abuse of a dangerous drug.

The Spaniards, however, encouraged coca abuse. After the Conquest, the number of *cocals*, "coca plantations," rose steadily. Each year coca growers forced thousands of Indians to work in the hot, damp lowlands of the Eastern Cordillera. Overworked and underfed, the Indians died in droves, only to be replaced by others. But the coca they produced was a bonanza for growers and mine owners alike. The growers made fortunes selling coca to the mine owners, who gave it to the miners, who died producing the silver that made Spain a world power. Coca addiction quickly spread beyond the mines, infecting the native population as a whole. It still does.

The Spaniards tried to conquer the Indians' souls as well as their bodies. As in their other colonies, the Spaniards wanted to make converts to Christianity. Yet they often went about it in the spirit of Francisco Pizarro rather than Bartholomé de las Casas.

Coca addicts. Unlike the Inca rulers, who limited the use of coca to the nobility, the Spaniards distributed coca leaves to miners to stimulate production. As a result, the coca-chewing habit spread throughout Peru, causing an addiction problem that persists until today.

Priests flocked to New Castile in the years after the Conquest. Some were patient men who took time to learn Quechua, the Inca language. It was through their efforts that Quechua became a written language, complete with dictionaries and grammars. Once the missionaries could speak to the people, they taught the people about Christianity and began to make converts. Many priests, however, were haughty, impatient men. It was they who herded villagers together for mass baptisms. It made no difference that the Indians understood nothing about Christianity. What

189

mattered was that they were pagans and must be converted whether they liked it or not.

Once Indians became Christian, they could never turn back. It was like crossing an invisible line into a topsy-turvy world. All their familiar gods had suddenly become "devils" and "demons." Suddenly all that had given them self-respect became evil. By losing their independence, the Inca lost their entire civilization.

To prevent them from sliding back to paganism, whatever reminded them of their past would be destroyed. Native religious leaders were jailed, whipped, or killed. Quipus, called "books of the devil," were burned, thereby erasing centuries of Inca history; those seen in museums today are but meaningless bits of string. Temples were torn down or rededicated as churches. Sacrifices were outlawed along with "instruments of idolatry," articles used in religious ceremonies. These articles ranged from musical instruments—drums, flutes, cymbals—to feather capes and animal masks. All were burned. All huacas and idols were destroyed. Some Spaniards believed themselves chosen by God for these works of destruction. Father Francisco de Avila, for example, burned over thirty thousand idols within a few years. It was even forbidden to dance the ancient dances and sing the ancient songs, crimes that brought three hundred lashes with the whip. To punish backsliders, priests might have their own prisons, whips, and chains. Yet there were also humane priests who urged good treatment for the natives. In the 1500s, these were usually the only Spaniards who defended Indian rights.

Still the Indians refused to abandon the faith of their ancestors. Although the Spaniards destroyed huacas wholesale, others always took their place. Indians worshipped the mountains and hills, the streams and lakes. These were creations of Viracocha, Lord of Beginnings, and would endure forever. The silver mines, even the city of Potosí itself, became huacas. Indians also hid old beliefs in Christian disguises. When pagan and Christian festivals fell on the same date, the Indians used the occasion to worship their old gods. Often small animals were sacrificed and sticks stained with their blood were buried in churches. In one church, hundreds of such sticks were found under the altar, which was secretly worshipped as a huaca.

Francisco de Toledo, viceroy from 1569 to 1581, took action. Toledo, one of Spain's leading noblemen, was an experienced soldier and government official. Strong-willed and hard-bitten, he knew what he wanted and how to get it. "To learn to be Christians," he said, "[Indians] must first learn to be men, and be introduced to government and the . . . reasonable way of life. . . . It is not possible to convert these Indians nor to make them live in a civilized way without removing them from their hideaways." This meant that they must be "reduced to towns." Work would begin on new towns and, when they were completed, local people would be moved there from their villages. The idea was to uproot the Indians from familiar surroundings, making it easier to control them and collect the work tax.

Beginning in 1571, natives were herded into Toledo's towns. In one district alone, two hundred villages were reduced to thirty-nine towns. In time, 1.5 million people were resettled, mostly by force. To prevent their returning, their home villages were burned.

As with the Sapa Incas before him, the viceroy meant to crush freedom of thought and action. Since the door of each house opened onto the street, his police could watch the goings-on inside. From birth to death, the most private details of the Indians' lives were regulated. Polygyny was outlawed, as were brother-sister marriages. No longer could parents name their children after birds, animals, or natural objects. It became a crime to deform babies' heads. Everyone had to go to church regularly, or they were fined or whipped. The dead could no longer be mummified, but had to be buried in the earth, where they'd decay. Neighbors were encouraged to spy on one another and to report rule-breakers to the authorities.

Viceroy Don Francisco de Toledo forced the Inca to move into towns and crushed the native rebels at Vilcabamba.

Toledo realized that as long as a Sapa Inca remained free, the Indians would hope for eventual freedom for themselves. By crushing the rebels of Vilcabamba, he'd crush the Indians' hopes and make them obedient subjects forever.

His countrymen had already made a start with Manco. After Almagro the Lad's defeat at Chupas, seven of his men fled to Vilcabamba. Manco's officers wanted to kill them immediately, but he treated them as honored guests; anyone who'd helped kill Francisco Pizarro was a friend of his. They remained with him for two years. But when Blasco Nuñez Vela arrived in Peru, the

Spaniards decided to win a pardon for their crimes. And what better way to do this than by killing the rebel Inca!

One day, about the middle of 1544, they rushed Manco during a game of horseshoes and stabbed him from behind. Running from the scene, they leaped on their horses and galloped toward Cuzco. They rode all day. Then, missing the road in a forest, they made camp for the night. Manco's men found them the next morning. Titu Cusi, Manco's nine-year-old son, years later recalled their capture. Some were pulled from their horses; others, retreating to a building, were burned out. Those who escaped the flames were speared as they ran. "All had to suffer very cruel deaths and some were burned."

But Manco was no more. For nine years he'd defied the power of Spain. Forced into the wilderness, he'd learned guerrilla warfare by trial and error. Defeated again and again, he'd always returned to the fight, wiser and tougher than ever. After he died, there were three more Sapa Incas, but they were puny creatures with none of Manco's wit or courage.

Before Manco died, he named his eldest son, Sayri Topa, his successor. The name means Royal Tobacco; the Indians used tobacco as a medicine, although they didn't smoke it. Sayri Topa felt that his cause was hopeless, that he'd never drive the Spaniards from Peru. When they offered him a pardon and the promise of an easy life, he accepted. He became a Christian in 1559 and left Vilcabamba. This time, at least, the Spaniards kept their word. They treated Sayri Topa as a king, albeit a powerless one, and gave him an encomienda with thousands of Indians. He died within a year of his surrender.

His brother Titu Cusi remained in Vilcabamba as the new Sapa Inca. Titu Cusi continued guerrilla raids, but he was no soldier and soon tired of fighting. He had an informal truce with the Spaniards and even accepted missionaries. Although he became a Christian, he never left Vilcabamba. He died in 1571, leaving the throne to Tupac Amaru, a younger brother.

Tupac Amaru was the last Sapa Inca. Soon after his coronation, Francisco de Toledo decided to end Inca resistance permanently. A Spanish army, spearheaded by Cañari scouts, invaded Vilcabamba with orders to destroy the rebels. That proved easier than anyone expected. For some unknown reason, the Inca failed to guard the mountain passes or to cut the suspension bridges. There was no real fighting; the Inca simply scattered, trying to escape along secret trails. Many did, but Tupac Amaru wasn't among them. He and his wife were found huddled next to a campfire, deserted by their followers. Also found were the mummies of Manco and Titu Cusi, which were burned.

Tupac Amaru was marched through the streets of Cuzco, led by a golden chain around his neck. He walked barefoot, head down, surrounded by Spaniards and Cañaris. Occasionally his guard let go of the chain and slapped Tupac Amaru's face. The humiliation was deliberate, for Toledo wanted to destroy the Sapa Inca as a symbol of Indian resistance. There was another mock trial, and Tupac Amaru was convicted of treason. The sentence was public beheading.

The viceroy wanted as many natives as possible to witness the execution, the better to convince them of Spain's power. Its date was set enough in advance to allow them to come from far away. People came in family groups, children clutching their parents' hands, old people hobbling. Clouds of dust rose above the columns, and their footsteps echoed across the valleys. They came to Cuzco, blowing kisses as their ancestors had done. Cuzco had changed since Francisco Pizarro first set eyes on it thirty-nine years before, but it was still the navel of the world, their greatest huaca.

On September 24, 1572, all eyes were on Cuzco's main square. Tupac Amaru was brought to the executioner on a mule draped in black velvet. He, too, wore black, and his hands were tied behind him. Cañari guards, eager to see his blood spilled, escorted him.

All windows facing the square were filled with Spanish on-

The last Sapa Inca. Tupac Amaru, barefooted, his head bowed, and a golden chain around his neck, being led through the streets of Cuzco. The Spaniard at the right carries an idol found in the Indian camp.

lookers. Indians crowded the square and climbed the roofs of houses; countless thousands watched from the surrounding hillsides. Arriving at the scaffold, Tupac Amaru dismounted, and a Cañari cut off his head with a sword.

As the executioner held up the head for all to see, the Inca fell to the ground, rolling and thrashing, shrieking and moaning. People beat their breasts and tore out clumps of their hair. The

195

Spaniards had slain a living god before their eyes and the pain of it was unbearable.

In the years that followed, the Inca not only suffered, they began to disappear. European diseases—typhus, measles, influenza—took a dreadful toll. Epidemics of smallpox raged for years at a time. The population fell by fifty percent in the thirty years following the Conquest, reaching 1.5 million in the 1560s. The Inca population kept falling until 1796, when it reached an all-time low of six hundred thousand.

Diseases, however, account for only part of the loss. The Conquest had reached into the Indians' souls, leaving them in despair. Their calm, orderly society had been shattered by a civil war, foreign conquest, a rebellion, and a series of civil wars among the conquerors. The wealth gathered over centuries had been wasted and the people enslaved. Their world had become a place of unrelieved misery. In the words of an Inca poet:

> *All things hide, all vanishes*
> *in suffering.*

Indians saw their Spanish masters as all-powerful devils, stone hearted and pitiless toward human suffering. Life lost its meaning, and they lost their will to live, or to bring new life into the world. The birthrate dropped. In their misery, Indians committed suicide and killed their children, said a Spaniard, "to free them from suffering." Often Indians declared that they didn't want to go to heaven if Spaniards were there, and because the demons in hell would treat them better.

The horrors of the Conquest are still vivid to the Inca. Even today, they relive it in their festivals and plays. One of these plays is about a mythical hero called Inca-ri. In the long-ago time, when people were happy, Inca-ri was killed by a white chieftain with a black beard. The chieftain cut off his head and buried it near Lima. But that head is not dead. It grows underground and will

196

return, complete with its body. When it does, the Land of the Four Quarters will be restored and the Inca will live forever in peace and happiness.

Peru's Indians are still among the poorest people in the world. Yet some believe that Inca-ri's body is growing, and that it will rise from the earth one day soon.

SOME
MORE BOOKS

Anderson, Charles I. G. *The Life and Letters of Vasco Nuñez de Balboa.* Westport, CT: Greenwood Press, 1970.

Anon. *The Conquest of Peru as Recorded by a Member of the Pizarro Expedition.* New York: The New York Public Library, 1929. Published in Seville in 1534, this, the first printed account of the Conquest, was written by one of the conquistadores who returned with Hernando Pizarro.

Ashburn, P. M. *The Ranks of Death: A Medical History of the Conquest of America.* New York: Coward-McCann, 1947.

Baudin, Louis. *Daily Life in Peru under the Last Incas.* New York: Macmillan, 1962.

————. *A Socialist Empire: The Incas of Peru.* New York: Van Nostrand, 1961.

Bierhorst, John. *Black Rainbow: Legends of the Incas and Myths of Ancient Peru.* New York: Farrar, 1976.

SOME MORE BOOKS

Bram, Joseph. *An Analysis of Inca Militarism.* Seattle: University of Washington Press, 1941.

Brundage, Burr Cartwright. *Empire of the Incas.* Norman: University of Oklahoma Press, 1963.

——. *Lords of Cuzco: A History and Description of the Inca People in Their Final Days.* Norman: University of Oklahoma Press, 1967.

——. *Two Earths, Two Heavens: An Essay Concerning the Aztecs and Incas.* Albuquerque: University of New Mexico Press, 1975.

Burland, C. A. *Peru under the Incas.* New York: G. P. Putnam's Sons, 1967.

Casas, Bartholomé de las. *History of the Indies.* New York: Harper, 1971.

Crosby, Alfred W., Jr. *The Columbian Exchange: Biological and Cultural Consequences of 1492.* Westport, CT: Greenwood Press, 1977.

Flornoy, Bertrand. *The World of the Inca.* New York: Vanguard, 1956.

Gibson, Charles. *Spain in America.* New York: Harper, 1966.

Hanke, Lewis. *The Spanish Struggle for Justice in the Conquest of America.* Boston: Little, Brown, 1965.

Hemming, John. *The Conquest of the Incas.* New York: Harcourt, 1970.

Hyams, Edwards, and Ordish, George. *The Last of the Incas: The Rise and Fall of an American Empire.* New York: Simon & Schuster, 1963.

Katz, Friedrich. *The Ancient American Civilizations.* New York: Praeger, 1974.

Leon, Pedro de Cieza de. *The Incas.* Norman: University of Oklahoma Press, 1959.

Lockhart, James. *The Men of Cajamarca: A Social and Biographical Study of the First Conquistadores of Peru.* Austin: University of Texas Press, 1976.

————. *Spanish Peru, 1532–1560: A Colonial Society.* Madison: University of Wisconsin Press, 1968.

Lothrop, S. K. *Inca Treasure as Depicted by Spanish Historians.* Los Angeles: n.p., 1938.

Markham, Clements R., ed. *Narratives of the Rites and Laws of the Yncas.* New York: Burt Franklin, n.d.

Means, Philip Ainsworth. *Fall of the Inca Empire and the Spanish Rule in Peru, 1530–1780.* New York: Gordian Press, 1964.

Metraux, Alfred. *The History of the Incas.* New York: Pantheon, 1969.

Parry, J. H. *The Spanish Seaborne Empire.* New York: Knopf, 1966.

Pizarro, Pedro. *Relation of the Discovery and Conquest of the Kingdom of Peru.* Boston: Longwood Press, 1977.

Prescott, William Hickling. *The Conquest of Peru.* Many editions of this book, first published in 1847, exist. It, together with his *The Conquest of Mexico,* are classic accounts of the destruction of the greatest of the American Indian civilizations. Both are beautifully written, holding the reader's interest from beginning to end.

Rowe, John H. "Inca Culture at the Time of the Spanish Conquest." *Handbook of South American Indians.* Ed. Julian H. Steward. Washington: Smithsonian Institution, 1946. 2: 183–330.

Sancho, Pedro. *An Account of the Conquest of Peru.* Boston: Longwood Press, 1978.

Sauer, Carl O. *The Early Spanish Main.* Berkeley: University of California Press, 1966.

SOME MORE BOOKS

Stearn, E. Wagner, and Stearn, Allen E. *The Effect of Smallpox on the Destiny of the Amerindian.* Boston: Bruce Humphries, 1942.

Vega, Garcilaso de la. *The Incas: Royal Commentaries of the Inca Garcilaso de la Vega.* New York: Avon, 1981.

von Hagen, Victor Wolfgang. *The Ancient Sun Kingdoms of the Americas.* New York: World Publishing Co., 1961.

Wachtel, Nathan. *The Vision of the Vanquished: The Spanish Conquest of Peru through Indian Eyes, 1530–1570.* New York: Barnes and Noble, 1977.

Zarate, Augustin de. *The Discovery and Conquest of Peru.* Baltimore: Penguin, 1968.

INDEX

INDEX

INDEX

INDEX

INDEX